# BUNRAKU

PERFORMING ARTS OF JAPAN: I

# BUNRAKU

## The Puppet Theater

by Tsuruo Ando

with an introduction by
Charles J. Dunn

A WEATHERHILL BOOK

WALKER/WEATHERHILL, *New York & Tokyo*
IN COLLABORATION WITH TANKOSHA, KYOTO

This book was originally published in Japanese by Tankosha, Kyoto, under the title *Bunraku*. The present text has been translated and adapted for Western readers by Don Kenny.

FIRST EDITION, 1970

Jointly published by John Weatherhill, Inc., of New York and Tokyo, and Tankosha of Kyoto / Distributed in the Far East by JOHN WEATHERHILL, INC., 7-6-13 Roppongi, Minato-ku, Tokyo 106, and in the United States by WALKER AND COMPANY, 720 Fifth Avenue, New York, N.Y. 10019 / Copyright © 1967, 1970, by Tankosha. Printed in Japan

LCC CARD No. 76-98332

# Table of Contents

# BUNRAKU

# Bunraku: An Appreciation

## by Charles J. Dunn

IT IS OFTEN SAID that Bunraku is the most advanced puppet theater in the world, and I am fully in agreement with this statement. There are many reasons why this should be so. To summarize them: it is so because Bunraku presents a serious, adult drama which uses a very high standard of artistic skill and is equal in status to that performed by living actors.

In the case of the British Isles there are, it is true, puppet plays, but they are usually for the entertainment of children. One genre of these takes its name from the principal male character, Punch, and his wife Judy and is known as "Punch and Judy." The plot is always the same cruel story of murders and appears to have given children a great deal of enjoyment in the past, but now it is considered too old-fashioned and is scarcely ever performed. In addition to this, one of its roles is played by a living dog called Toby, and it cannot be considered as a pure puppet theater. Among puppet theaters more modern than "Punch and Judy" there are some in the programs like "Watch with Mother" on television, but these too, it goes without saying, are directed toward the juvenile audience. Performances for adults sometimes turn up in cabaret shows and the like, but the content of these usually reminds one more of conjuring tricks, and they are quite unable to reach the high level of Bunraku.

3

Puppet theaters on the continent of Europe take many forms, and among them are such well-known ones as the French Grand Guignol and the comical performances by the Russian master Sergei Obraztsov, but they all exist with the object of either startling the audience or making it laugh, and so it is quite certain that they do not reach the standard of drama in the strict sense of the term. To divert the discussion from Europe to Asia, I have not yet had a chance to watch the Turkish and Indonesian shadow plays, but I gather that they are very impressive, particularly the *wayang*, performed as it is in the hot tropical night in Java. These Asian performances very often have varied plots and are of great interest, but their shadow puppets are after all only two-dimensional, and I imagine the Bunraku puppets are much more effective.

Of the three elements which make up Bunraku—namely, the chanter, the *shamisen* accompaniment, and the puppets—I consider the chanter and his narration the most important. There is good reason for this opinion, since the narrative chanting, called Gidayu or Gidayu-bushi, is a form of entertainment in itself and can be performed without a theatrical setting. I think that both historically and artistically the chanting is the basic art in Bunraku.

The profession of telling tales has existed in most countries throughout the world. The Scottish and Irish bards and the like, who told their tales to the accompaniment of the harp or the fiddle, the ancestor of the violin, are one example of this. When I was in Moscow in 1960, I had the opportunity of listening to several local performers who had come from Central Asia and among whom there were some who had a remarkable talent for chanting the legends and heroic tales of their native regions. In some respects Gidayu can be considered as one phenomenon out of many that exist throughout the world, but at the same time it is very different from the chanting that exists in other places. The difference can be summed up by saying that the Japanese chanting is *shibui*—that is, it tends not to use colorful effects but to be restrained—whereas in other places the normal tendency is toward the vivid and the spectacular. I should like to elaborate upon this point by drawing upon my own experience.

It often happens that I have to lecture to students of London University and others on the subject of Japanese drama. In particular, when I am talking about Bunraku, I use as illustrative material color slides, gramophone records, and two Bunraku puppet heads that I have in my possession. All the students who attend these lectures admire the skill of the craftsmen who made the heads, with their very effective mechanisms working the eyes and mouth. On the other hand, they have great difficulty in appreciating the Gidayu records—or at least the greater part of them. Some passages, it is true, are not so difficult as others. For example, in the play *Shimpan Utazaimon*, in the scene at the village of Nozaki where the heroine is rowed off in a boat, there is a very cheerful duet for *shamisen* with a jaunty rhythm which anyone could understand and take pleasure in. And in the play *Hadesugata Onna Maiginu*, in the scene at the wineseller's, the musical phrase that starts the *sawari*, as the heroine wonders where her erring husband is, is preceded by six melancholy notes played on the *shamisen* which are capable of stimulating the imagination of whoever it might be—and, in fact, stimulate that of my students. In a word, when the *shamisen* music is of the sort that has a definite melody or establishes a mood, even Westerners who are not accustomed to listening to it can derive pleasure from it. In these circumstances the Gidayu *shamisen,* with its special faculty for stirring men's hearts, is particularly attractive.

But the chanting of Gidayu is another matter, and there are many difficulties connected with it. It might be thought that the greatest obstacle to the comprehension of Gidayu by foreigners would be that they do not understand Japanese, but it is possible that this is not so at all. Opera fans are quite accustomed to listening to singers performing in a language that they themselves do not understand and to judging the excellence of their performance; so the language problem may not be so great as one might think.

No, the real difficulty is the voice and the method of enunciation of the Gidayu chanter. Westerners appreciate the clear Italian or German type of voice such as they hear in performances of opera or art songs, coming through the open throat, but the hoarse Gidayu voice production, growled out through the constricted throat, they find most unusual and difficult to understand. In addition, when they hear that these same chanters, as young men, had voices that Westerners might very well have thought beautiful and that, as their skill improved with the passage of the years, their voices lost what Westerners would consider their beauty and became standard Gidayu voices, they have, it seems, a feeling that somehow or other this is to be regretted.

In fact, when on a recent occasion I played a record of some Bunraku chanting to a group of schoolteachers who had never heard it before, one of them was so shocked that he said: "It spoils God's work." There is a strong feeling, especially in Britain, that it is wrong to change nature and that anything unnatural or artificial is to be avoided. If I may be allowed, for the moment, to leave Bunraku and mention flower arrangement, I should like to point out that many foreigners, especially people from Great Britain, find Japanese flower arrangement difficult to understand because so often the flower stems, or even the flowers themselves, are twisted and distorted into shapes which they do not have in nature. The British, of course, are famous for their horror of cruelty to animals, even though this horror might often appear hypocritical to people from other lands. But it is not only animals to which one must not be cruel. It is also flowers, so that the more advanced examples of Japanese flower arrangement, even though they are recognized as making beautiful patterns, may, sentimentally but not logically, be found displeasing because they seem to involve "cruelty to flowers." In the same way (and I apologize to the reader for having strayed from the subject), to a Westerner who has not been initiated into the true appreciation of the art, the hoarse tones of the Gidayu chanter may seem to be an example of cruelty to human beings.

Moreover, it is no good merely listening. With many Western singers, it is a positive advantage not to be able to see them, for their singing is often accompanied by what are apparently inevitable facial distortions that go a long way toward spoiling the pleasure of their audience. For singers of this sort, the performance on a gramophone record or on radio is ideal. But if one really wants to progress to the level of being able properly to understand Gidayu, one must allow it to come in not only through one's ears but through one's eyes as well. After a considerable period of listening and watching, one realizes the degree of variety that is possible in order to fit the various roles. The West, too, has had in the past skillful chanters or tellers of tales. I have mentioned the minstrels of old, whose art must have been very much like that of the *biwa-hoshi*, their counterparts in Japan, but in more recent times also there have been great public readers. The famous novelist Charles Dickens developed the reading of his works into a real art form, which he performed on theatrical stages both in England and abroad. But, although no doubt he put great feeling into his readings, there was no musical side to his act, and it is very unlikely that the range of voices that he used was as great as that of a Gidayu chanter. For, in the case of the chanter, the same one man can take any possible part. No matter what the role may be—woman or man, old or young, a virtuous man or a villain—all sorts of voices are produced from just the one throat, and that is not all, for he has to take the part of the chorus as well.

The conversational passages are performed in a realistic style, and they are all skillfully done, but since the voice is the typical Gidayu voice, my feeling is that the most successful role type is that of the middle-aged villain. An excellent example of this is the role of Moronao in *The Faithful Forty-seven*. His wickedness is portrayed most clearly in the scene in the palace, where he taunts his unfortunate adversary into drawing his sword against him, not only by his words but also by the powers of expression of the hoarse voice that enunciates them. He sounds far more evil than a villain in a Western opera, for however wicked an opera villain may be, his voice must remain beautiful.

Again, though the Gidayu performer's profession is that of a chanter, he has partly to be an actor. The only thing that he is unable to do is to move away from the place where he is sitting. He grips the reading stand at which he sits, he causes expressions of all kinds to flow across his face, he crouches down or straightens up, and thus he supplements with the movements of his body the emotional force of the words he utters and compensates for the deficiencies of the dolls' powers of expression.

I should like to add one more word about the chanter. If one really wishes to appreciate his art, one must be able to chant some Gidayu oneself. If one is able to do even a little "grunting," one can not only hear it with one's ears and see it with one's eyes but can also experience it with one's whole body and enjoy it through one's abdominal muscles (it is said that the Gidayu voice comes from the belly, the Western voice from the head) and through the pain in one's throat. It is, of course, much the same with Noh plays. Unless one has learned a little Noh singing or Noh dancing, one cannot be expected to have a full understanding of what it is about. In the West a certain fraction of the audience for concerts of music are performers in their own right, and there are often spectators who follow the music from a printed score in much the same way that people watching Noh plays read the *utai-bon* (librettos) in order to follow the play and improve their own performance of Noh chanting. Western audiences, however, have for the most part done scarcely any of the sort of performing they are watching, which means that the particular muscular appreciation one can get from Noh and Bunraku is lacking to them. In Bunraku, and even more in Noh, one is not there merely to be entertained, for there is a sort of audience participation—not, it is true, in the normal sense of the word but nonetheless of very great significance.

The *shamisen* player is very much the "anchor man." No matter how excited the chanter and the doll manipulators become, he remains unmoved and plays meticulously on. As he plays, he utters little cries and grunts, and they keep the whole performance going at its correct rhythm. The resemblance between him and a top-class accompanist to some singer in Western style is very close. Neither is there just to play the notes in a mechanical sort of way, but they both help the interpretation to an extent greater than the general public may realize. They defer to an artist of skill and experience but give great assistance to someone just starting his career. They are unobtrusive and leave all the fireworks to the vocalist, but at the same time they make one feel that they are persons upon whom one can place the greatest reliance.

It should be remembered that the Gidayu *shamisen,* with its thick post, is for use in a theater and produces a loud noise. Nevertheless it is flexible enough to provide an accompaniment suitable for any emotion that may be required. It is true, however, that the most impressive moments occur when several Gidayu *shamisen* are being energetically played in unison. This I find a very stirring sound, as capable of arousing excitement as a fanfare of trumpets.

Yet, however much I may express my personal view that the chanting is the fundamental part of Bunraku, the ordinary members of the audience will presumably not think so. When they go into the Asahi Theater in Osaka, which is the home of Bunraku, the really interesting thing that attracts their attention is the puppets.

When I saw Bunraku for the first time, it looked like a confused crowd of men and dolls, and it was difficult to sort out who or what everybody was, but only a short time was required to become used to it, and soon the human beings became almost invisible, and the dolls seemed to be moving about by themselves. This impression is of course strengthened by the traditional and basic way of doing things, whereby the manipulators wear black clothes and black hoods.

The dolls can hardly be said to possess a body. What they do have is something like a basic framework over which their clothes are put on. The only thing that gives the doll's body its three-dimensional roundness is the way these clothes are arranged. It is only when the feet of the doll have a reason for being visible that they are attached. Men's feet can be seen, and so dolls playing male parts always have feet, but in the case of female parts the dolls normally wear long kimono, and the movement of the feet is represented by moving the bottom of the kimono skirt in an appropriate manner. In special circumstances—for example, when the part is that of a young girl like the pilgrim in *Yugiri at the Straits of Awa*—feet are used for female dolls.

Puppet arms and hands are of many kinds, and different ones are used according to the role being played at the time. For example, when a puppet is made to play a musical instrument, it is made to hold the appropriate plectrum, be it for the *shamisen*, the *biwa* (lute), or the *koto* (horizontal harp), and it is possible to have a device worked by strings whereby the five fingers can be manipulated so as to bend or straighten out independently at the joints, which are in the same places as those of human hands. However, such complicated mechanisms as this are used only when there is a real necessity for them.

This limitation of stage devices to the requirements of the situation demonstrates one of the characteristics of the Japanese theater: economy of method or, to put it in other words, the principle that something complicated should not be used if something simple will do, that anything which is quite unnecessary might just as well be abandoned. If a house is erected on the stage, the question of whether or not a gateway will be put up for the house depends entirely upon whether or not there is to be any action at the gateway. And if, during a scene, a point is reached where the gateway is no longer going to be used, the black-clad stagehands normally come out and take it away.

In the same way the faculty of movement is given to the dolls' hands only to the extent that it corresponds to necessity, and the puppet is provided with only those parts of its body that will have to show. In fact, in situations where it would be altogether too much of a complication if something was done with the doll's hand, the manipulator puts his own hand out from the sleeve of the doll's clothing and does whatever needs to be done, such as gripping a sword or a fan. When both hands have to be used, the actions of two manipulators have to be coordinated, and this entails a great deal of cooperation on their part.

It is the head which gives each doll its individuality. Man or woman, old or young, good or evil, warrior or townsman—all distinctions depend upon the head, although not on its shape alone, for it is possible to fit any one head with a variety of wigs. Thus, by the skillful combination of head and clothing, hands and feet, it is possible to cover a very large number of roles.

The actors in the live traditional theater, the Kabuki, apply makeup of various sorts, such as white for women and young male lovers and fixed color patterns (*kumadori*) for certain other male roles. In the case of the Bunraku puppets such coloration is applied permanently, and since the dollmaker can make the heads with idealized features, it follows that a suitable head can be found for any part, whereas a live actor is to some extent restricted by the features that are his by nature. In Bunraku, fearsome men are really fearsome, beauties are really beauties, villains are outright villains. Another point of interest is that although Bunraku puppet heads vary in size in accordance with the types of roles for which they are intended, generally they seem somewhat small in proportion to the whole doll. In fact, as a result of the great reflecting power of the lacquer used to paint the faces of the dolls, the audience is led to feel that the heads are larger than they really are. It is an indication of the skill and sophistication of the Japanese craftsman that this is taken into account.

The Bunraku heads that I have been describing up to now are only those of the puppets taking principal roles. There are other types as well. One of these consists of the heads used when special effects are required. For example, there is one with two faces which looks, from the front, like a beautiful woman but which, when it is turned around and the hair is pushed over backwards, becomes a fox. Or, to show a face suddenly becoming covered with blood from a wound, one can fix, over a face previously smeared with some red color, a mask with the same features as the face underneath. Then, when the wound is received, the mask is whipped off and the blood-stained face appears. This trick is extremely effective. But these are merely devices to astound the audiences and are not of very high class from the artistic point of view. They resemble, in fact, some of the tricks that are used in Western marionette theaters, where the object is to show not a natural action but the sort of things that can be done only by puppets, such as dances by skeletons that can disarticulate and rearticulate.

A type of head which I think is of somewhat greater interest is the one called the *tsume*. The roles played by dolls with heads of this type are usually those of the lower orders, such as farmers and the soldiery, and the dolls themselves are usually of a simple variety, manipulated by one person only. In comparison with the glistening well-polished heads of the puppets taking the main roles, the *tsume* are crude but at the same time show a character of comicality, of honesty, and of humanity. The ancestors of the *tsume* existed in the simple puppets that were used in the earlier part of the seventeenth century, and their brothers still survive on the island of Sado among the so-called *noroma* puppets that are used in short comic interludes between more serious dramas. It is possible that the *tsume* are classifiable as "pop art." Whenever these cheerful dolls appear, I, for one, am very pleased, but it may be just because I am very fond of the comic element, and in my opinion there is no doubt that from the artistic point of view the most outstanding doll type is the *oyama* or female doll.

I remarked earlier that the role most suited to the Gidayu chanters is that of the villain, such as Moronao in *The Faithful Forty-seven.* In Kabuki I cannot help feeling that the highest position is occupied by the roles of "good" men like that of Sukeroku in the play of the same name, Benkei in *The Subscription List,* or—to name one that was originally a puppet-play role—Jihei the paper merchant in *The Double Suicide at Ten no Amijima.* It is indisputable that the art of actors taking female roles in Kabuki is superb, but I feel in my heart that the really representative Kabuki role is the sort of male role that I have mentioned. I think that the Bunraku puppets which take female parts are far more feminine than their Kabuki counterparts, but it is probable that other people will have different ideas on the subject. This is another instance, perhaps, of the dislike of the unnatural that the Briton often feels. The Kabuki *onnagata* (female impersonator) has something about him that is masculine, even though it may be only the hands and feet. The female puppets, however, especially in *sewa-mono* (plays dealing with the lives of commoners), give an idealized picture of womanhood. Everything about them is feminine—their faces, their clothes, their way of walking, and, in particular, their hand movements. As I have suggested before, one would expect that the existence of three manipulators for each doll would mean that the movements on the stage must become very confused and incomprehensible, but in fact this does not usually happen. Perhaps it has some connection with the gentleness of Japanese women, for one might even have the fancy that the female puppets cooperated with or even identified themselves with their manipulators.

The following incident happened one day when I was watching a rehearsal at the Asahi Theater. For some reason or other the foot manipulator who was helping in the handling of a young female doll went off somewhere else. The poor doll  was thus deprived of the power of walking, and as the time approached for her to move away from where she was, she turned her head from left to right in a searching gesture. When at last she had discovered where the manipulator was, she stretched out her own hand and beckoned him to her side. My readers will certainly think that I am suffering from an excess of imagination, but this true story demonstrates the degree to which the manipulator feels that his puppet is an extension of himself. When the role is that of a man, normally of course there exists the same cooperation with the manipulators as I have imagined for the female doll, but it sometimes happens that when a villain becomes aggressive and starts thrashing about he seems really to acquire a life of his own and to be trying to escape from the manipulators' grip.

In 1950, when I saw Bunraku for the first time, the principal  manipulator very often did not wear a hood but appeared in what is known as the *dezukai* style—that is, with his head and face in full view. At times he wore splendid-colored clothes. Severe critics of Bunraku assert that the use of *dezukai* should not be allowed because it diverts the attention from the puppet to the manipulator. There is no doubt that in principle this assertion is correct, but my personal sentiment in the matter is that I feel some gratitude to the *dezukai* system. Although the puppets are possessed of all sorts of abilities, there is a restriction on the extent to which their faces can show emotion. The principal manipulator strives to express the emotions being felt by the puppet through the movements of its body, and in order to do this he uses the professional technique of causing an expression to cross his face which matches the emotion being felt by his puppet. If he is wearing a hood, his facial expression is concealed from the audience, but when he appears in *dezukai* style it becomes completely visible. Some people, especially Japanese purists, may find this sort of thing something of an obstacle to their full enjoyment, but for someone like myself who has not achieved complete powers of comprehension in Japanese, this method is very helpful. What I mean is that I try to obtain from all possible sources hints upon how to enjoy the performance, and I get quite a lot of assistance from the principal manipulator's face.

Up to this point I have been examining the three elements of the Bunraku performance separately. When one goes to join the audience at the Asahi Theater, however, one does not take in each element separately but enjoys the complete performance as a whole—and all at once. The chanter, the *shamisen* accompanist, and the doll manipulators all work in cooperation with each other. One often hears it said that with Bunraku one does not get bored. When there is a lot going on, through the ears there come in the sounds of the *shamisen*, the cries and grunts of the *shamisen* player, the voice of the chanter, the rhythmical stamping of the foot manipulators, and, occasionally, grunts from the manipulators themselves. Through the eyes one has the dancing of the puppets, the changing expressions on the face of the principal manipulator if he is working in *dezukai* style, and the movements of the chanter. Even in quieter moments there is activity in two separate areas of sight and sound, so that there is always something to see and something to listen to.

At this point I should like to indulge in some generalization and some consideration of dramatic theory and discuss the question of the function that the puppets fulfill in the Bunraku performance. That is to say, are the puppets supposed to be actually saying the words of the play or not? No matter where in the world a particular puppet theater comes from, if the person who actually speaks the words is placed out of sight, then the puppet must be recognized as an actor in the full sense of the word. In this case it is allowable for the puppet to be seen as really talking. It might even be something like ventriloquism. However, if the chanter is in full view of the public, what is the situation then? When one watches the performance of the Gidayu chanter, sitting there for all the audience to see, one gets the impression that, except for the fact that he is not allowed to walk about, he is operating just like an actor.

I think that it is the chanter who speaks the words in addition to performing his function of narrating the "chorus" parts— that is, setting the scene and commenting on the action. If this is so, what are the puppets doing? I believe that they are in a sort of auxiliary position, with the object of establishing what sort of characters are appearing, what these characters are doing, and what they are feeling. Another interpretation is possible—namely that the chanter serves as a third party, an intermediary, to explain the actions of the puppets to the audience. Were the present-day Gidayu chanters to perform less emotionally, this might very well be the correct interpretation.

At all events, there are opportunities, from time to time, to see Bunraku on television in Japan. During these broadcasts the chanter is not shown on the screen, and the manipulators are scarcely visible. It becomes an interesting program very suited to television presentation, but I think that it is very different from the complete Bunraku that one can see at the Asahi Theater.

There are, generally speaking, two sorts of plays in Bunraku: *jidai-mono* (historical dramas) and *sewa-mono* (domestic dramas). The latter are very often love dramas, but it is very rarely—perhaps never—a case of falling in love and getting married, as it might be in the West. In the Tokugawa (Edo) period, romantic love tended to be the seed of tragedy. In the representative domestic drama of the period, *The Double Suicide at Ten no Amijima,* the paper merchant Jihei falls in love with one of the town prostitutes and becomes so obsessed that he is ready to abandon everything for her sake. But the rules of Tokugawa society make such a thing impossible, and finally they commit suicide together. Such domestic dramas are given an extremely realistic presentation, and the depiction of human character in them is very skillful and accurate. As I have noted before, the female characters in these plays are very well matched to the construction and manipulation of Bunraku puppets, and my personal opinion is that among them are to be found the masterpieces of the Bunraku theater.

In historical dramas, too, the theme of the conflict between love and duty is a favorite one. Whereas in the domestic dramas one has the collision between individual emotion on the one side and the honesty of a merchant or responsibility toward one's parents or one's wife and children on the other, in the historical plays the opposition tends to be between one's duty to one's

2. *Mountain scene from* Proper Upbringing of a Young Lady at Mount Imose

*3. Scene from* The Dumpling Sellers

*4. Scene from* Fishing for a Wife

5. *Ichiriki Teahouse scene from* The Faithful Forty-seven

6. *The courtesan Yugiri in* Yugiri *at the Straits of Awa*

master or one's parents and one's affection toward wife and children. The supreme objective of these dramas was to defend the contemporary morality, and, as a result, things always turn out tragically for the erring individual. Modern persons, especially foreigners, feel that all this is an infringement on human rights, but what were the motives of the writers at the time? One of their purposes was probably to arouse sympathy in the audience for these pathetic characters and to make the spectators weep. It seems to me that the Japanese are fond of weeping, and, provided that they could have the pleasure of being made to shed tears, people were ready to go to the theater in considerable numbers and pay their entrance fees.

As I watch Bunraku plays and Kabuki plays derived from Bunraku, I often wonder if the grief shown by some of the characters when they have sacrificed the objects of their affection in order to preserve the ties of loyalty was, in fact, when the play was written, a sort of protest—an effort, however indirectly and inexplicitly expressed, to have the inhumanity of the feudal system rectified. Did the plays that have the conflict between *giri* (duty) and *ninjo* (human feelings) as their theme actually have as one of their objects the amelioration of the situation, so that human beings of low rank in the social scale would have the right to place their personal feelings above the loyalty that they owed to their lords? It is tempting to think so, but I cannot believe that one of their purposes was to bring about a reform of social conditions.

The criticism is often made by Japanese, not Westerners, that the themes of Bunraku are old-fashioned and feudalistic and that, for this reason, there is nothing to be gained from watching the plays, but if one considers the plays of Shakespeare one sees that the same sort of question arises. In his historical pieces there are many scenes of great cruelty, but one does not say that one will not go to see them because of the existence of these scenes. One's object is purely to judge objectively the skill, or lack of it, of the actors and the methods of production. Bunraku should be viewed in the same sort of spirit.

Up to now I have been discussing the very high world status of Bunraku, its components, and the art as a whole. Now, however, I should like to spend a little time considering the position that Bunraku holds in relation to the other traditional Japanese theatrical arts.

The twofold system of puppets and chanter is fundamental to Bunraku. The actions are performed by the puppets, but the dialogue and the explanatory chorus are the function of the chanter. This sort of system also exists in the Noh plays. In these, at certain times, the words that one would expect to be spoken by the *shite* (principal actor) are sung by the chorus, which also has the function of explaining and commenting upon the circumstances of the action. In other words, in both Bunraku and Noh there is an intermediary between the actor and the audience, and the assumption of a mask by Noh actors signifies that they are not the real characters that appear in the story but are only representing them for this particular performance. In the same way, Bunraku puppets are not the human characters but merely represent them. The above statements would seem very obvious to Japanese readers, but they are of great significance in the consideration of the theater as a world-wide art.

I feel that here there is a considerable difference from the realistic "theater of illusion" that flourished in Europe until about twenty years ago. This theater, in almost the same way as the cinema, appears to have tried to make the audience think that a room on the stage was a real room and that the characters who appeared in it were real people and not actors. No such thing as this exists in Noh or Bunraku. It may be that seventeenth-century Kabuki had the possibility of becoming such a theater, but in the eighteenth century almost the whole range of puppet plays entered Kabuki. From then on, the influence of Bunraku on Kabuki has remained very strong. The greater part of the Kabuki repertory is taken from the puppet plays, the technique of the actors in these pieces is based on that of the puppets, and there are a small number of scenes in which people appear on the stage as manipulators. It may be that Bunraku is the only puppet theater in the world that has employed techniques advanced enough to exert a serious influence upon live acting.

A reverse influence from Kabuki to Bunraku is not entirely nonexistent, especially in pieces that were originally Noh plays which entered the Kabuki repertory as dance pieces and then moved on to become puppet plays. Then again, along with the revolving stage, Bunraku on occasion uses that other great Japanese invention, the *hanamichi*—the raised passageway from the rear of the auditorium to the stage—which also originated in Kabuki. But my opinion is that the sight of a crowd of people manipulating dolls on the *hanamichi* in the midst of the audience is not attractive. When they appear on the stage, the rail that divides the stage from the audience conceals the lower half of the manipulator's body, and the effect is much more pleasing. Perhaps I am overstrict, but my personal feeling is that plays that were originally Bunraku plays should be played on the Bunraku stage and that those intended for Kabuki should be restricted to Kabuki.

Bunraku now receives support from the National Theater and the Ministry of Education, and it seems that it is able to play only pieces that do not compromise its artistic conscience. Bunraku is unique in world theater. Should it disappear, the theater of the whole world would suffer a great blow. It is therefore important that it be preserved not only for the sake of Japan alone but also for the world in general.

# BUNRAKU

CHAPTER 1

# The Black Stage

IN WINTER THE GULLS fly over the water of the Sakurada moat around the Imperial Palace while the silent gray stone embankment stands sentinel in the background. In front of this moat, set a little back off the street behind a grove of rather scrawny newly planted pine trees, stands the new National Theater of Japan. It is an imposing structure built in the ancient *azekura* style of the famous Shoso-in treasure house at Nara.

The small hall which forms a part of this structure has become the Tokyo home of Bunraku. It is a charming little theater which seats slightly more than six hundred people. During a performance of Bunraku it comes to life with a feeling of perfect harmony.

Whenever Bunraku is performed in Tokyo, I take my daughter to see it. I don't force her to go with me; she always asks to be taken. I had always hoped she would grow up to be a person who appreciated the classical arts of her own country such as Bunraku, Kabuki, and the music of the *shamisen*, but at the same time I made it a point never to force these things upon her. Even so, one day she came to me and said, "Daddy, I want to see Bunraku."

Actually one should say "hear," not "see," Bunraku since the narrator's chant called Gidayu-bushi is the most important part of the performance. But my daughter, who had never had any

33

contact with this art, was more attracted to "seeing" the dolls. Of course this is as it should be.

This took place only two or three years ago, soon after my daughter had graduated from all the schools one is expected to attend in the process of growing up. I took her to see her first Bunraku, extremely happy that she had asked to go completely of her own free will. When I suggested at the end of the matinee that we come back to see the evening performance another day, as she was probably rather tired, she insisted that we stay and see both programs. During the performance, I stole an occasional glance at her face. The more impressed and excited she became, the more happy and satisfied I became. Some time after that, when the National Theater was completed, with the first theater in history specially built for Bunraku in Tokyo, my daughter was as happy as though it had been built in her own back yard.

Every time we see Bunraku together, she asks numerous questions during the intervals and sometimes even during the performance itself. The more intelligent her questions, the prouder I become of the vast knowledge and sensitive feeling for the arts she has gained. My pride in her tends to exaggerate the actual extent of her knowledge to the point that I sometimes catch myself about to answer, "What? You don't know that yet?" when she asks a more basic question than usual.

At first she was particularly interested in the basic construction of the stage itself. As for color, the keynote of the stage is black—not a shiny glaring black, but a soft smoky black that absorbs light. The house lights during a performance are lowered a little more than during Kabuki, giving a sort of twilight effect. One takes one's place in the rows of comfortable medium-brown seats and finds the curtain called *joshiki-maku* before

*8-9. The warriors Abe Sadato and Abe Muneto in* On the Adachi Plain in Oshu

*10–11. Two episodes from* The Tale of Sugawara Michizane

14   *Mitsuhide in* The Picture Book of the Taiko Tales

15. *Misao in* The Picture Book of the Taiko Tales

*16–19. Four episodes from the Kawazura Mansion scene in* Yoshitsune and the Thousand Cherry Trees

*20–23. Four episodes from the Sushi Shop scene in* Yoshitsune and the Thousand Cherry Trees

*24. Yuranosuke in* The Faithful Forty-seven

*25. Enya Hangan in* The Faithful Forty-seven

*26. Fukashichi and Omiwa in* Proper Upbringing of a Young Lady at Mount Imose

32–34. *Three episodes from the Horikawa Monkey Trainer scene in* A Recent Story of Rivalry in Kawara

*37–38.  Two episodes from the Warm Kotatsu and Autumn Rain scene in* The Double
Suicide at Ten no Amijima

*39–40. Two scenes from* The Miracle at Tsubosaka

*41–44. Two episodes from The Tale* of the Summer Festival in Osaka

45. *The courtesan Akoya in* The Chronicle
of the Battle Helmet at Dannoura

one's eyes. Across the stage in front of this curtain runs a ledge about ten inches high decorated with a simple geometric pattern. Both the ledge itself and the pattern on it are black, in shades just different enough for the pattern to be distinguishable from its background. This ledge is called *san-no-tesuri*. It has no practical use at present but is always part of the decoration which can be seen in front of the curtain.

When the curtain opens, the *ni-no-tesuri* and the *ichi-no-tesuri* come into view behind. The *ni-no-tesuri* is directly behind the *san-no-tesuri*, while the *ichi-no-tesuri* is at the very back of the stage. The *ichi-no-tesuri*, also called the *hon-te*, is the support for the main set in front of which the dolls perform. These are the basic elements of the Bunraku stage.

As stated above, the *san-no-tesuri* seems to have no practical purpose except perhaps to hide the bottom edge of the curtain. But the presence of this low black board running in a perfectly straight line across the front of the stage seems to lend a sense of order and discipline to the atmosphere which is evident in every Bunraku play. For this reason, I feel that even though it serves no practical purpose, it holds a very important position in this traditional Japanese art.

As one takes his seat in the theater before the curtain rises, the most conspicuous thing that meets the eye is the small platform placed outside and to the right of the stage proper. It is a revolving stage about eight and a half feet in diameter with a standing screen in the center. This screen is covered with gold paper in front and silver in back, both surrounded by a wide black frame. The narrator, called a *tayu*, and his *shamisen* accompanist are seated side by side on this small stage in front of one side of the screen. They are brought into view with a sharp half-revolution of the small stage as the curtain is raised on the main stage. This small stage, called the *yuka,* is of course very important to Bunraku.

When viewed from the audience, the *tayu* with his highly decorated reading stand is on the left, and his accompanist is on the right-hand side. In most cases only one *tayu* and one *shamisen* player are used, but when more appear, an additional platform of the same height is added at the left of the main stage. These platforms are painted with the same smoky black as the *san-no-tesuri* and also have a similar, but more complicated, geometric pattern across the front.

Behind the curtain, as we have noted above, is the *ni-no-tesuri,* another rail-like piece of scenery which runs all the way across the stage a little higher than the *san-no-tesuri.* It is either of unpainted wood or has some light-colored design as part of the set, and thus it serves to soften the effect of the stern black line of the *san-no-tesuri* and set off the action of the puppets, adding greatly to the total effect.

The *tayu* and his *shamisen* accompanist are always dressed in the formal costume of the Edo period (1603–1868), which consists of the stiff upper garment called a *kataginu* and the trouser-like *hakama* over a plain black kimono. To the right and left of the two men are tall candlesticks which give a calm, traditional effect to their appearance and are symbolic of their demanding art.

# CHAPTER 2

# Gorobei from Tennoji

IN A DISCUSSION of the traditional art called Bunraku, the dolls are of course important, but first it is necessary to tell of the origin of Gidayu-bushi, the chanted narration of the drama, and how it developed into the form with which we are familiar today.

The fourth year of Keian (1651) was a year of public unrest in Japan, particularly in Edo (present Tokyo). The third Tokugawa shogun, Iemitsu, died. Yui Shosetsu's* conspiracy against the government was discovered. Shosetsu committed suicide in Sumpu (present Shizuoka), and his accomplice Maruhashi Chuya was arrested in Edo.

During the same year, in a village near Osaka called Tennoji, a son was born to a farming family. In time, he was to become famous as Takemoto Gidayu, originator of Gidayu-bushi, but nothing in his early years—except perhaps his resonant voice— indicated that he was marked for celebrity. He grew up, became a farmer like his father, and was known as Gorobei from Tennoji. Every day he went to work in his field at Yasui, which was situated at the foot of Mount Tenjin, not far from his home in Tennoji. This seems to have been just a few steps east of the east gate of the present Shitenno Temple.

On the mountainside almost directly above Gorobei's rice

* All Japanese personal names in this book are given in Japanese order: surname first, given name last.

paddy was a restaurant and tea shop called the Tokuya. At that
time Tennoji boasted eight famous tea shops, among which the
Tokuya held a proud position. It commanded a splendid view
from its perch on the mountainside. Below it lay Mount Osaka,
with the Kiyomizu River flowing nearby, and behind it on the
upper slopes stood the forests of Mount Tenjin. The Tokuya also
had its own garden, famous for its exquisite beauty throughout
the four seasons of the year.

The owner of the Tokuya, Kiyomizu Rihei, was an accomplished performer of *joruri* (narrative singing accompanied by
the *shamisen*) in the style of the Inoue school. He was also known
as a man of many interests and was highly adept at all the pas-
times of the upper classes, including the tea ceremony, flower
arrangement, the songs of the Noh drama, the game of *go,* and
poetry. He was considered a man of elegant taste and was the
toast of Osaka. Rihei had also been born in Tennoji. When the
famous *joruri* narrator Inoue Harima-no-jo (1633–85) retired
from the stage, Rihei succeeded him, becoming Harima II. Men
of taste and position were always visiting Rihei at the Tokuya
to take Inoue-school *joruri* lessons and to enjoy the flowers in the
spring and the moon in the fall.

The document called *Ayatsuri Nendaiki* tells us a little about
what the style of Harima-no-jo's *joruri* must have been like. It
states that stories of valor and the death of brave warriors which
were particularly effective in exciting feelings of grief and tears
were the main subject matter. His style seems to have been one
in which the musical tones and rhythms were very precise and
which was very strict on pronouncing the words, so that they
would be easily heard and would make the story clearly understood by all present. The melodies were so clear and tuneful that
they became the popular songs of the day.

Gorobei from Tennoji was probably a boy of about twenty when he began to take note of the melodies floating down from Rihei's rehearsals and lessons in the Tokuya up on the cliff above his rice paddy. Before long, Gorobei had memorized the stories and would sing along with the voices overhead as he tilled his small field.

A *joruri* narrator in those days had a rather special position in society—a definite prestige. He was considered one of the elite. Gorobei longed to become a real *joruri* narrator. But he had never heard of a mere farmer attaining this exalted position. Becoming a *joruri* narrator would mean that he could add the title *soregashi* to his name as Kabuki actors did. But, unlike a Kabuki actor, he might some day be recognized by the emperor and be given the even higher title of *jo*. This would give him a social distinction, definitely setting him apart from the common riffraff. The trend of the times had created a situation in which any man who had an appreciable talent would become a *joruri* narrator to attain a high social position, since it was not possible to do so in any of the other performing arts.

What, exactly, is *joruri?* It has already been defined above as narrative singing accompanied by the *shamisen,* but let us look for a moment at its origins. The name is actually that of a fictional princess, heroine of *The Tale of Princess Joruri* (Joruri-hime Monogatari), an old romance said to have been written before 1485. It was this tale that originally furnished the most popular pieces for musical narration. In fact, the beautiful dreamlike love story of Princess Joruri and the hero Ushiwaka-maru was as big a hit as any popular song or TV drama might be today. The musical narratives and the art of presenting them thus came to be known as *joruri,* and the name continued to be used even after stories from other sources were added to the repertoire.

This narration, which was originally a one-man show, first added the *shamisen* as accompaniment, and later, during the Edo period, the puppets were added. Development along the same line in the years to follow produced the narrated puppet dramas we know today as *ningyo* (puppet) *joruri* or more commonly as Bunraku. This period of development will be explained in more detail later on in the book.

Right now let us get back to our friend Gorobei from Tennoji. One day his talent and great desire to become a narrator came to the attention of Rihei. Today we would say Gorobei was "scouted."

It was the hottest part of the hottest day of the year. Gorobei had just finished his lunch and was relaxing in the shade of a tree near his rice paddy. He decided to practice the Inoue-school narration he had by now learned to perfection by listening to the lessons going on up above while he worked.

His voice was splendidly loud and clear. His high notes were precise and unstrained. His low notes had a full-powered resonance. His handling of the material was rich in emotional depth and at the same time in perfect taste. Many amateurs and professionals flocked to the Tokuya every day for lessons, but there was no one among them who could match the inborn qualities of Gorobei's voice.

Rihei happened to hear this early-afternoon performance as he was trying to find relief from the heat in a room on the second floor of his home high up on the mountainside. He immediately sent for the owner of this marvelous voice. When Gorobei was brought before him, Rihei immediately asked, "Would you like to become a professional narrator?" Gorobei answered simply and without hesitation, "I would."

 There is no record of how long Gorobei had been mimicking

Rihei's narration as he worked in his rice paddy, but he was discovered by Rihei in 1671 at the age of twenty and seems to have made his first appearance on the stage as a professional only three years later, in 1674. Records clearly show that he was an assistant narrator in Rihei's troupe from the time it began performing at the Dotombori theater in Osaka. Eventually, however, Gorobei became dissatisfied with the *joruri* style of the Inoue school. He discussed the problem with Rihei, gained his permission, and went to Kyoto for further study.

At that time Uji Kaga-no-jo (1635–1711) was very popular in Kyoto. Kaga-no-jo was the last narrator of the older style called *ko-joruri*. He had begun by learning Noh and had later taken up *joruri*. His *joruri*, while based on that of Inoue Harima-no-jo, also included techniques from many other forms of song and narration popular at the time—for example, Noh, *heikyoku*, and *kowaka*—and the result was an extremely beautiful and pleasant style. Gorobei had been trained in the hard, stern style of the Inoue school called Harima-bushi, but he now set his mind on learning this softer Uji style.

Looking back to the previous generation, we find an interesting progression. There had been a *ko-joruri* narrator in Edo named Satsuma Joun (1593–1672). He had learned *joruri* from Sawazumi Kengyo (dates of birth and death unknown) and had then gone to Edo, where he learned the puppet-play methods from Sugiyama Tango-no-jo (dates of birth and death unknown). Combining these two aspects, he had doubled his popularity.

Joun's style was particularly hard and strong compared to that of Tango-no-jo. Joun had a student named Toraya Genda-yu (dates of birth and death unknown) who was active in Edo from the Kanei (1624–43) till the Genroku era (1688–1703). His style was brash and showy like all other forms of Edo art during this period. At one period in his life, Gendayu had spent some time in the Osaka-Kyoto area. Two of his talented students had remained, Inoue Harima-no-jo in Osaka and Uji Kaga-no-jo in Kyoto.

Gorobei mastered the styles of Harima II (Rihei) and Kaga-no-jo. To these styles he added every song and sound he could find—from ceremonies and sermons to folk songs, popular songs, and even the calls of the market place. He gathered and studied anything and everything that might in any way add to his range of technique and expression.

In 1677, at the age of twenty-six, Gorobei narrated the second act of *The Tale of Saigyo, the Poet-Priest* (Saigyo Monogatari), known as "The Burglary of the Lay Priest Fujisawa" (Fujisawa Nyudo Yato), with Kaga-no-jo's troupe. He received high praise for his flashy masculine style and his strong clear voice, which carried like the crack of a whip to every corner of the theater. His enunciation was of such clarity that even the beginning and ending syllables were clear as a bell and easily understood by everyone present. He immediately became the talk of the town. Before long Gorobei left Kaga-no-jo's troupe and changed his name to Kiyomizu Ridayu.

# CHAPTER 3

# Gidayu-bushi Is Born

THE AYATSURI NENDAIKI, the same book that tells of Ridayu's great success in his performance of *The Tale of Saigyo, the Poet-Priest,* also tells of the hard time he had after he left Kaga-no-jo's troupe and tried to perform on his own at Shijo-gawara in Kyoto. Always resourceful, Ridayu finally found himself in a real dilemma. But his luck soon changed for the better when he became acquainted with Takeya Shobei. Shobei had been in business with a narrator called Kidayu, but they had recently broken up their partnership, and Shobei was looking for someone to start a new troupe with.

Ridayu joined forces with Takeya Shobei, and they added a blind master *shamisen* player named Osaki Gon'emon to their troupe. Gon'emon had been accompanist for Inoue Harima-no-jo, and since Harima-no-jo's death he had been accompanying one of Harima-no-jo's former students. This is what he was doing when he was hired by Shobei and Ridayu. Thus Ridayu reached maturity in his art and gained the best possible impresario and an excellent accompanist all at the same time. It seems that Ridayu and Gon'emon must have gotten along very well together both personally and artistically because they continued from that time to perform together till Ridayu's death more than thirty years later.

Kiyomizu Ridayu thought it best to get away from Kyoto for a time; so the little troupe of three set out on a tour together. It

75

was a long lonely trip through the western part of the country. They reached Itsukushima in Aki (commonly known today as Miyajima, near present Hiroshima) in the spring and, since they attracted better than usual crowds, decided to settle there for a time.

Ridayu was a very religious man. Every day as soon as the performance was finished, he would go to the Itsukushima Shrine to pray. A legend tells us that one evening after he had performed the purification rites, he was sitting in quiet meditation, with his eyes lightly closed, on the dancing stage of the shrine, facing the huge red *torii* (shrine gate) that seems to grow right up out of the sea. The waves lapped softly underneath the floor of the stage. Before long the moon came out and bathed the surface of the water with its gentle beams.

Ridayu was lost in a sort of spiritual ecstasy, not knowing whether his eyes were open or closed, whether he was sitting or standing, or even exactly where he was. While he was in this state, the tide came in, making the whole shrine seem as though it were actually afloat on the water. Ridayu began to hear music. Then he saw a cherub rise up out of the water wearing a heavenly crown and a scarlet robe. It came toward Ridayu and gave him a scroll, which he gratefully received. Then the cherub disappeared, the music faded, and he awoke from his dream. Ridayu took this as a sign from heaven directing him to create his own unique style of *joruri*.

This story is of course only a legend, but I like it because it seems so appropriate to Ridayu's style of *joruri*, known today as Gidayu-bushi or simply Gidayu. In 1684 (some say 1685) Ridayu perfected his new style and changed his name to Takemoto Gidayu. Thus the style has come down to us under the name of its originator.

Ridayu had very specific reasons for changing his name to Takemoto Gidayu. First of all he considered the concept expressed by the character *gi* (義) in "Gidayu" the highest virtue a human being could possibly possess. *Gi* means to have dignity, which in turn means to walk the road of truth, to obey the just rules, to always do the things one should do and never do the things one shouldn't do. Man must maintain the five cardinal virtues: justice, benevolence, wisdom, politeness, and fidelity.

Justice, expressed by the character *gi*, was considered the most masculine of all the virtues. Thus during the early part of the Edo period it was expected to be the most important part of the moral code of any man of position from the time he reached maturity. Justice is also very much a part of the strict art of *joruri*, as are all the other virtues.

In this change of name, Rihei also expressed deep gratitude to Takeya Shobei. He used the first character of Shobei's last name, *take*, and the character *moto*, which means origin or fountainhead, to form his new last name, Takemoto.

Ozeki Gon'emon also borrowed one character from Shobei's last name and one from his teacher Sawazumi Kengyo's last name, changing his name to Takezawa Gon'emon. (The "s" becomes "z" for purposes of euphony.) Since Sawazumi Kengyo is considered to have been the originator of *shamisen* accompaniment for *joruri*, the character *sawa* from his family name has always been used in the professional names of *shamisen* accompanists since that time. Toyozawa, Nozawa, Tsuruzawa, and Hanazawa are some of the more famous of these.

About this time at Dotombori, in Osaka, prosperous theaters were lined up one after another, presenting varied programs including *joruri*, Kabuki, magicians, and puppets. In February (some say May) 1684 a huge banner called a *yagura-mon* was hung from the turret on top of one of the theaters in Dotombori. The pattern on this banner was Takemoto Gidayu's family crest, and under the banner was a sign almost covering the front of the theater on which was written in bold yard-high letters just one name, Takemoto Gidayu.

This was the birth of the theater called the Takemoto-za. As the name indicated, the owner, director, and main performer of this theater was Takemoto Gidayu himself. The event marked the beginning of a long line of succession in Bunraku which continued all the way down to Toyotake Yamashiro-no-shojo, who died in 1967 at the age of eighty-eight.

Gidayu was thirty-three at this time. His first performance in his new theater was a five-act play entitled *The Heir of the Soga Family* (Yotsugi Soga), which had been written originally for Uji Kaga-no-jo by Chikamatsu Monzaemon (1653–1724). His performance of the second and third acts, which depict the long lonely trip of the courtesan Tora no Shojo, was particularly fine. This play established his popularity in Osaka, and the name Takemoto Gidayu was on everyone's lips.

The play was especially appropriate as a sort of celebration of the launching of Gidayu's career, for it told of the birth of Suke-waka to Tora no Shojo after the death of the famous Soga brothers, and of Sukewaka's restoration of the house of Soga to its former glory. Chikamatsu himself was quite satisfied with this play and proud of it. Its felicitous theme and the good fortune it brought to Gidayu gave positive proof of its worth as well as of Gidayu's great talent.

Nowadays when a full-length play is given, a narrator performs only one section of one act. The best and most difficult section of each act is the last scene, which is the climax of that part of the story. The best narrator in the troupe always performs his favorite among these sections in each performance, but never more than one section. Gidayu had almost legendary endurance. He performed this most difficult part of all five acts in every performance: the end of the first act, called *daijo;* the same part of the second, third, and fourth acts, called *kiri;* and the especially difficult and exhausting *o-zume* of the fifth act. This was a phenomenal feat of endurance which would be absolutely unthinkable today.

Puppets had been used since the days of Kaga-no-jo to supplement and make the narration more interesting. The first master puppeteer was Yoshida Saburobei (?–1747), who became famous along with Gidayu at the Takemoto-za. According to a magazine of that time, Saburobei was particularly skillful in the handling of male puppets. He was also the man who developed the system used today in which each puppet is handled by three men, one handling the head and right arm, another handling the left arm, and the third handling the legs. Saburobei's son Yoshida Bunzaburo (?–1760) contributed greatly to the development and refinement of this system. Another early puppeteer, Tatsumatsu Hachirobei (?–1734) was famous for handling female puppets.

# CHAPTER 4

# The Hearts and Minds
# of the Artists

OTHER NARRATORS IN Takemoto Gidayu's troupe besides himself
were Michinoku Modayu, Takemoto Tanomo, Takumi Ridayu,
Takemoto Naniwa, and Takemoto Kiyodayu. Takezawa To-
shiro was a master *shamisen* player who had grown up under
Gon'emon's training and was also a member of this troupe.
The gathering of all these excellent performers in one troupe was
of course achieved partly through Takeya Shobei's skill as an
impresario, but it was mainly Takemoto Gidayu's popularity
and his strong appeal that brought them together.

All the performers gathered every day at the Takemoto-za
before sunrise and had their three meals together at the theater.
Gidayu considered that the spirit of togetherness created by the
sharing of all their meals was necessary in order to maintain and
further develop the high quality of their art. As soon as breakfast
was over, they all refreshed and cleansed their bodies and spirits
with a steaming bath in the dressing room. They started each
day in the clear morning air, fresh from the bath and dressed in
crisp costumes for the day's performance. The first piece of
clothing put on was a long waistband which was wrapped firmly
around the abdomen to give added strength and endurance to
the muscles which support the voice.

Backstage each performer in turn carried out simple purifi-

80

cation rites and said a prayer. The strict cleanliness of body and spirit practiced by these artists must have had at least some influence on the stagehands and other backstage assistants. We may imagine that they went about their own tasks with uplifted hearts and renewed energy, setting up the stage and contributing their part to the progression of the drama unfolding there. This total atmosphere no doubt played a major role in bringing about the highly artistic production that was to be seen at the Takemoto-za. Gidayu must have planned this system of respectful etiquette in order to bring his art to the level of honor and spiritual dignity of which he dreamed. These signs of respect are still part of the tradition of Bunraku today.

One time I counted the number of times a narrator bows in humility or reverence from the time he begins dressing until he finishes his narration and leaves the stage. It came to five times in all. First, after putting on the white socks called *tabi*, he receives the long cotton waistband explained above. While it is still folded, he raises it above his head, lightly bows to it, and closes his eyes in prayer for a moment. He seems to be asking the waistband for its help in giving him additional strength for the day's performance.

Even though this waistband looks like the average sash worn on the outside to keep the kimono in place, it is actually much more. As we have noted above, it plays such an important part in breath control and strengthening of the lower abdominal muscles that it becomes almost a part of the body. Thus the respect paid to it in this bow is only logical.

The waistband is wrapped securely in place, and the rest of the costume is put on over it. The last part of the costume to be put on is the stiff vestlike *kataginu*. An assistant places the *kataginu* on the shoulders of the performer with the long wide bands called *tare* hanging down in front. The narrator receives one band in each hand, places them one on top of the other, raises them above his eyes and bows once more, then pulls them down straight underneath his kimono sash.

Next he puts on the broad trouserlike *hakama* and seats himself on the large cushion on the half of the small revolving stage which is turned away from the audience. Then he receives a long, narrow pillowlike object filled with sand. He salutes it in the same manner in which he bowed to the waistband and the *tare* and then passes it through his sleeve and places it inside the front of his kimono above the waistband. This strange pillow is called a *futokoro*. During a performance, the narrator moves quite violently, so that a costume put on in the ordinary way would become quite untidy by the end of his appearance on the stage. The *futokoro* helps to keep the whole costume in place, especially the *tare*, which otherwise would slip up out of the sash and flop around unpleasantly. This one little accessory makes it possible for the narrator to look as neat as when he started, even after working up a sweat while experiencing the violent emotions and vigorous movements necessary in the telling of his story.

The cue is given, the small stage is revolved, and the narrator and his accompanist appear before the audience with heads bowed low. The oldest puppeteer in the troupe comes on stage in a black costume with a black veil over his face, and makes the announcement called *tozai*.

The buoyantly old-fashioned style of Hyoji Yoshida (1883–) cannot be beat. He has been the main *tozai* announcer for almost forty years now. I remember even back when I was a college student, I felt that it somehow didn't seem like real Bunraku unless Hyoji appeared for the *tozai*. The style which he has

46. *Painting: early puppeteers*

48. *Painting: early puppeteers*

47. *Painting: early hand-puppet show*

49.  *Painting: marionettes operated by strings*

50–51. Paintings: puppet theaters of the Keichō era

52. *Woodblock print: Kabuki actor
Sanogawa Ichimatsu as a puppeteer*

maintained is one of the small but important aspects necessary to the traditions of Bunraku.

The narrator and his accompanist maintain their deep bow till the *tozai* is completed. "Tozai! I hereby announce the performers for today. The narrator is ———, and his accompanist on the *shamisen* is ———. Tozai!" On the second cry of "Tozai!" they raise their heads and face the audience.

Next the narrator picks up the libretto which is on the ornate reading stand in front of him, lifts it above his head with both hands, and bows. This bow has three meanings: it expresses respect for the author of the play, it is a sort of prayer that the narrator's performance will be worthy of the work, and it expresses gratitude for the presence of the audience and a request that they listen to him.

The narrator replaces the libretto on his reading stand. As he opens it to the title page, the announcer utters his final "Tozai!" and the *shamisen* player begins the introductory music called the *okuri*. This introduction is very important in preparing the audience and setting the mood for each act.

When the act is finished and the last melody dies away, the narrator once again lifts the libretto above his head and pays his respects. I myself know of no other traditional art in which the performers maintain such a high level of decorum both in the process of a performance and in their daily lives.

These constant expressions of humility and gratitude, which at first glance seem bothersome to the utmost, actually serve to get rid of the unnecessary excitement and stagefright evident in any performing art and are thus a great help in regulating breathing and maintaining control. The strictly proper, settled atmosphere also makes itself felt in the audience and contributes to the creation of the special world of Bunraku. Noh is the only other traditional Japanese stage art which maintains and expresses anything like this spirit.

Gidayu must have been very much aware of what he was doing back in the Edo period when he set up this strict system of spiritual, mental, and physical discipline which is so impressive and effective to this day. Gidayu-bushi was from the beginning not mere entertainment but was created as an expression of ideals and a way of life. The whole story of the foundation of the art of Gidayu-bushi is told in the character pronounced *gi,* meaning dignity and justice, used by Takemoto Gidayu in his own name.

# CHAPTER 5

# Gidayu and the Takemoto-za

THE SUMMER FOLLOWING its opening, another Chikamatsu play was presented at the Takemoto-za. This time it was *The River Dyed Deep Blue* (Aisome-gawa); then, in the fall, came *The Tale of the Alphabet* (I-Ro-Ha Monogatari), which was also written by Chikamatsu. These plays were both in the *ko-joruri* style and had both been previously written for Uji Kaga-no-jo.

Gidayu was indeed an excellent performer, but this was not the only reason for his great success. In May of the same year (1684) occurred the death of Inoue Harima-no-jo II, one of the men who had split the world of *ko-joruri* in two. Thus Gidayu's only remaining rival was Uji Kaga-no-jo.

In January 1685, Kaga-no-jo came to perform in Osaka. Now the older *ko-joruri* style and Gidayu's newer style of *joruri*, which was later to become known by his name, came into direct competition for the first time, and the differences between them were plain for all to see.

Kaga-no-jo brought out a new play called *The Calendar* (Koyomi), which is thought to have been written by the great seventeenth-century novelist Ihara Saikaku. Gidayu's "secret weapon" was a new play by Chikamatsu entitled *The New Calendar and Lessons Learned by a Wise Woman* (Kenjo no Tenarai Narabi-ni Shin-goyomi). The reason why both Kaga-no-jo and Gidayu chose plays dealing with the calendar at this particular time was that the Tokugawa government had changed from the

93

lunar to the solar calendar just the previous March, making the calendar a favorite subject of conversation at that time.

The timing must have been perfect, for it became the fashion of the day to see and compare the styles of these two rivals who had previously been student and teacher. As soon as the newness wore off, however, Kaga-no-jo was severely criticized, attendance at his performances fell off, and finally he was forced to close down and return to Kyoto. The end result was complete victory for Gidayu.

This means that Chikamatsu's work won out over Saikaku's, but there were many reasons for the victory besides the works themselves. Gidayu used some sort of new stage-effect mechanism in the Chikamatsu play which amazed his audiences and contributed greatly to his popularity. It is not known exactly what this mechanism was, but it must have added a lot to the total effect of Gidayu's performance. Various other reasons are also given for his success, among them the natural preference of the people of Osaka for local performers and their love of the spectacular.

But Kaga-no-jo was not one to be beaten so easily. He came back to Dotombori in Osaka and opened with a play entitled *The Triumphal Return to Yashima* (Gaijin Yashima). This time he was very successful, but unfortunately the theater where he was performing burned down, and he was forced to give up and return to Kyoto once more. Kaga-no-jo never tried to compete with Gidayu again.

Gidayu's real establishment as the master of all *joruri* narrators actually came in 1686. He opened in February with a new play, the first that Chikamatsu wrote expressly for him, entitled *The Successful Kagekiyo* (Shusse Kagekiyo). Chikamatsu wrote this play in celebration of Gidayu's personal success and the popularity of the new style of *joruri* he had created. Up to this time Gidayu had always performed plays written for the older style of Kaga-no-jo. *The Successful Kagekiyo* provided the first opportunity to utilize the full range of Gidayu's talents.

The new play was based on the older dance pieces and *kojoruri* which handled the subject of the warrior Kagekiyo, and its pattern of composition influenced all later pieces written on this subject. The play also marked a turning point in Chikamatsu's career. His older pieces had all been in a strictly narrative style. Beginning with *The Successful Kagekiyo,* he wrote in a more and more dramatic style.

Gidayu continued to perform old and new plays by Chikamatsu as well as those of other authors, ever broadening his artistic scope. In May 1701 he was recognized for his achievements by the emperor and took the name Chikugo-no-jo. His full new name was Takemoto Chikugo-no-jo Fujiwara Hironori. This was an official title such as those given by the emperor in those days to townspeople, artists, and merchants who deserved special praise. In earlier days this sort of title would have given a man a great deal of power. There were four honorary name suffixes: *kami, suki, jo,* and *sakan.* Chikugo was the name of the area which is the present Fukuoka Prefecture in Kyushu. In the days before the militarists took control of the government, the title Chikugo-no-jo would have meant something like "Governor of Fukuoka Prefecture," but when Gidayu received this name, it was no more than an honor similar to the present-day knighting system in England. Even today the *jo* suffix in the name of a *joruri* narrator indicates the highest position within the world of Bunraku.

Chikamatsu wrote *Semimaru* for Chikugo-no-jo in honor of his fifty-first birthday. Semimaru was a legendary blind master of the *biwa*, the Japanese lute, and was revered as the god of music by the *heikyoku* performers. *Heikyoku* are narratives from the classical *Tale of the Heike* (Heike Monogatari) performed to the accompaniment of the *biwa*. Chikugo-no-jo's performance of *Semimaru* was received with such enthusiasm that lines from the libretto were taken up and sung by all and sundry as popular songs of the day. But the highest point in Chikugo-no-jo's popularity came in 1703 with his performance of Chikamatsu's play *The Double Suicide at Sonezaki* (Sonezaki Shinju).

The presentation of this play was a risky venture both for the Takemoto-za, which was in financial difficulties at the time, and for Chikamatsu, who had never before made an attempt to write in this style. As it turned out, *The Double Suicide at Sonezaki* was the first of a series of very successful plays based on actual events—stories of young couples in love who can find no way to be together honorably except in death. Plays of this type, dealing with the lives of contemporary commoners, are called *sewa-mono*, whereas plays treating older, more stylized historical themes are called *jidai-mono*.

The doll for the heroine Ohatsu in *The Double Suicide at Sonezaki* was handled by Tatsumatsu Hachirobei, a specialist in handling female puppets. His sensitive interpretation of the sadness of the bewitching courtesan moved the hearts of the audiences and added greatly to the popularity of the play.

With this play a new level of realism and pathos was reached in the art of Gidayu-bushi and the use of the puppets. It marked the beginning of a new era not only in the lives of Chikamatsu, Chikugo-no-jo, the puppeteers, and the Takemoto-za but in the history of Japanese theater as well. The great success of the play brought prosperity to the Takemoto-za, which had been operating in the red for some eighteen years. During this period, theaters which attempted to present programs of artistic interest almost without exception operated constantly in the red. Like artists of all ages and nations, Chikugo-no-jo had always been more interested in/the perfection and maintenance of his art than in making money.

Taking advantage of the success of the Takemoto-za, he retired from his position as overall head of the troupe in 1704 and began to spend his time pondering over religious writings, meditating, and working for the further perfection of his art. In 1705 Takeda Izumo (? 1747) took over as head of the troupe, shouldering the responsibilities which had been carried by both Chikugo-no-jo and Takeya Shobei, who also retired at this time. The Takeda family held this position for three generations.

Chikamatsu's *Battle of Kokusenya* (Kokusenya Kassen) is said to have been based on a story suggested by Takeda Izumo I. Izumo wrote two other successful plays himself: *The Five Daughters of Sansho-dayu* (Sansho-dayu no Gonin Musume) and *The Story of Ashiya Doman Ouchi* (Ashiya Doman Ouchi Kagami), and he was an absolute genius as an impresario.

After Izumo took over, the Takemoto-za became more and more successful, until it finally exceeded even the more spectacular Kabuki in popularity. Chikugo-no-jo, who had been the head of the Takemoto-za, was now its highest-paid performer, and Chikamatsu was officially hired as its main playwright. This situation continued for nine years, until Chikugo-no-jo's death in 1714 at the age of sixty-three.

A critic of that time compared Chikugo-no-jo's Gidayu-bushi with the earlier styles of Harima-no-jo and Kaga-no-jo, noting that Harima-no-jo had stressed the melodic line while Kaga-no-jo had concentrated on expressing the story line. Chikugo-no-jo, the critic said, transcended both of these older masters by bring-ing out every nuance of the melody, utilizing it to give an ever more sensitive interpretation of the story. He also incorporated and developed the overall dramatic rhythm pattern of the Noh drama called *jo-ha-kyu*—that is, introduction, development, and climax. The result of his attempts is the moving art we know today as Gidayu-bushi. Many years of strict discipline and passion for his art had changed the singing farm boy Gorobei from Tennoji to Chikugo-no-jo, the creator of a great art based on human justice and dignity.

*53.* Oshizumo puppets

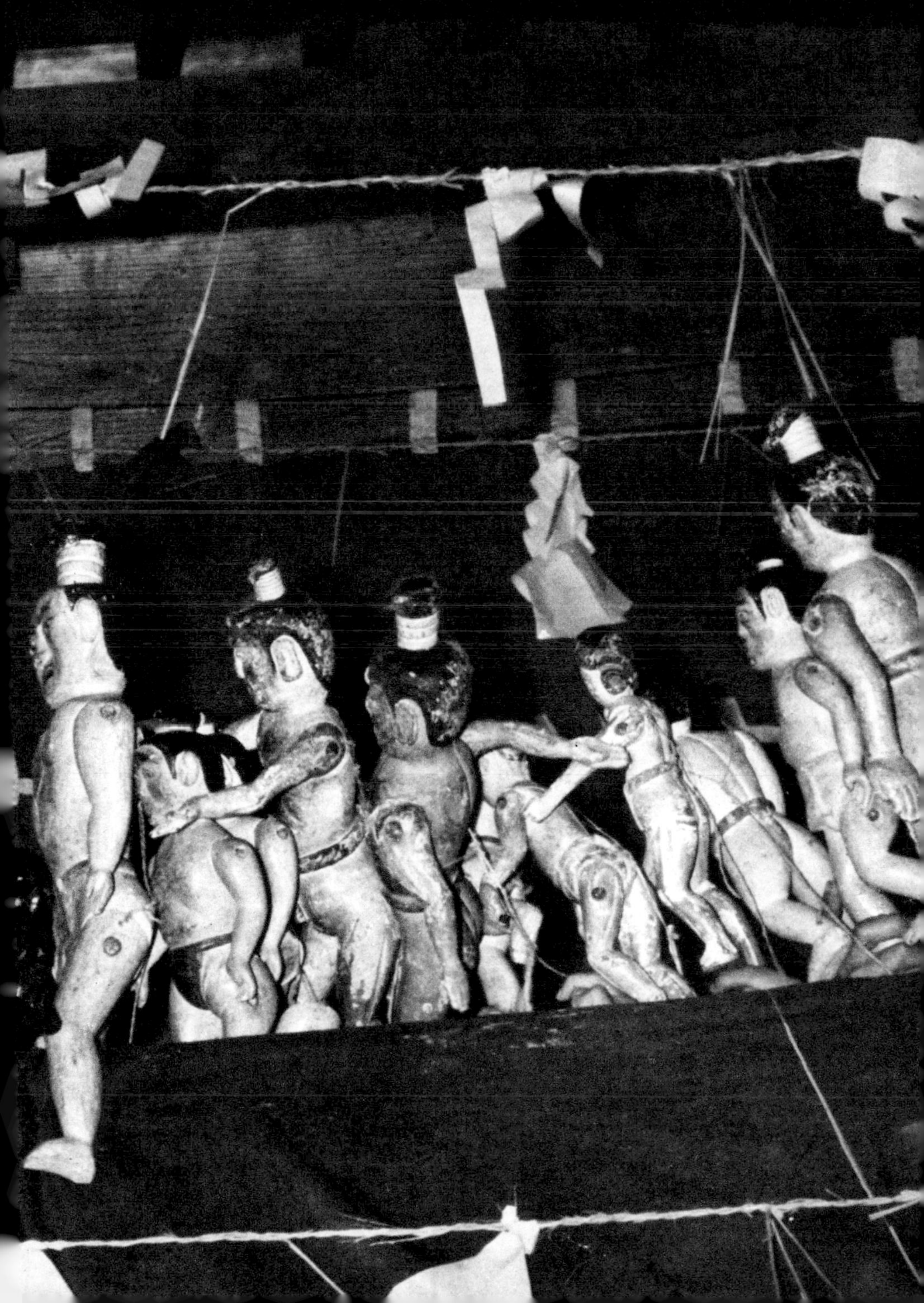

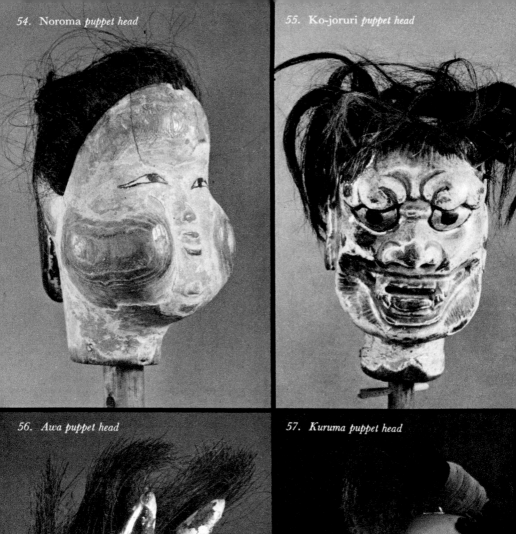

54. Noroma *puppet head*

55. Ko-joruri *puppet head*

56. *Awa puppet head*

57. *Kuruma puppet head*

58. *Dance puppet used in Koyo Shrine festival*

59. *Aizumo puppet used in Kohyo Shrine festival*

60. *Ko-joruri puppet head, male*

61. *Ko-joruri puppet head, female*

64. Drawing: Princess Joruri with musicians

65. Drawing: Princess Joruri

66. *Painting: puppet performance in front of a dry-goods shop*

67. *Painting: puppet play in the Kan'ei era*

68. *Painting : early puppet theater*

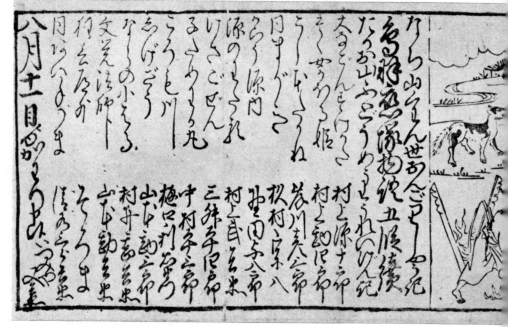

*69. Program for a puppet performance in the Kambun era*

*70. Drawing: dressing room of Yamamoto Tosa-no-jo's troupe*

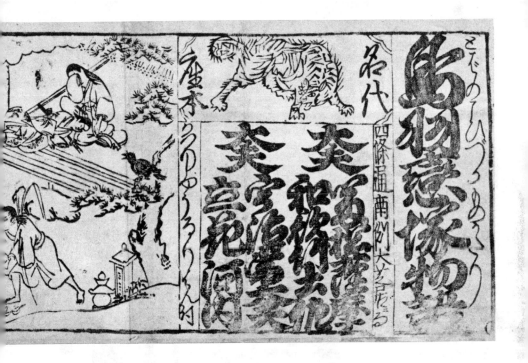

71. *Caricature depicting exploits of hero Kimpira*

73. *Drawing: performance by Uji Kaga-no-jo's troupe*

75. *Portrait of Takemoto Gidayu*

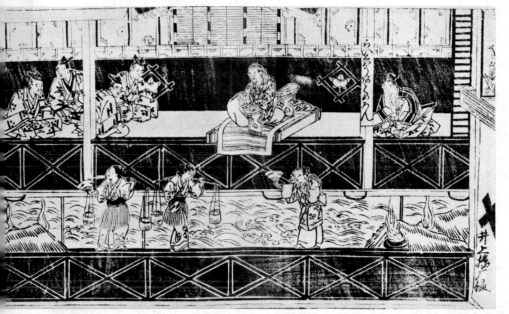

74. *Drawing: performance by Inoue Harima-no-jo's troupe*

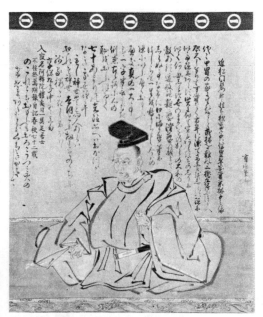

76. *Portrait of Chikamatsu Monzaemon*

77. *Drawing: premiere performance of* The Tale of Hojo Tokiyori

79. *Drawing: stage tricks devised by Takeda Izumo I*

78. *Drawing: the Toyotake-za and the Takemoto-za*

80. *Drawing: performance of* **The Double Suicide at Sonezaki**

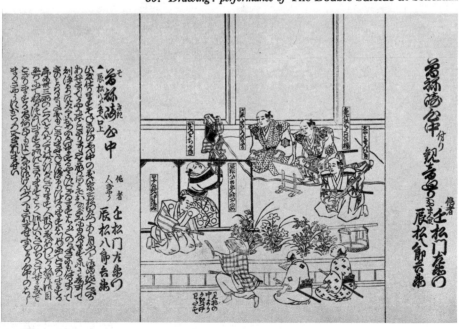

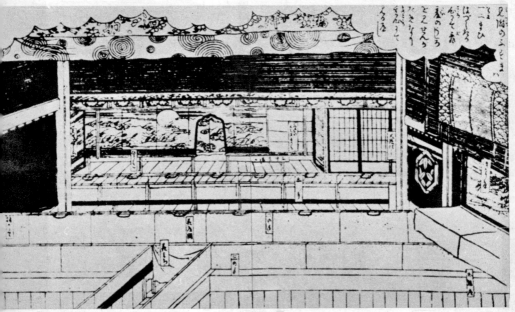

81. *Drawing:* joruri *theater of the Kyowa era*

82. *Drawing: early three-man puppets*

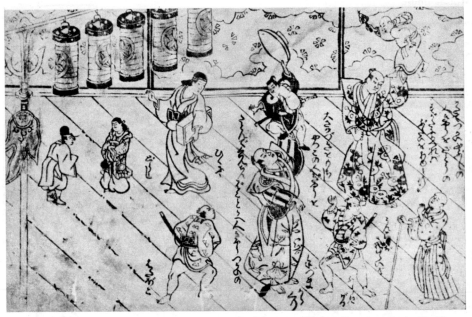

83. *Drawing from program for a puppet show in the Kan'en era*

84. *Drawing from program for a puppet show in the middle Edo period*

**85.** *Program for premiere performance of* Proper Upbringing of a Young Lady at Mount Imose

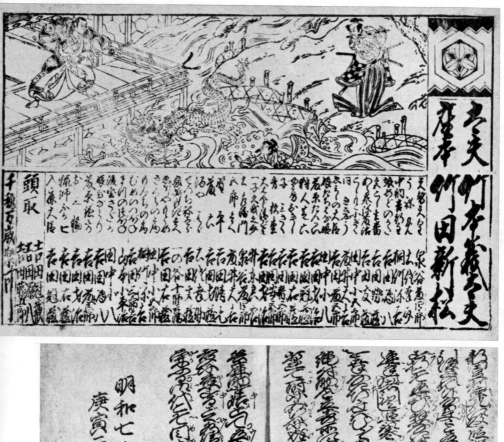

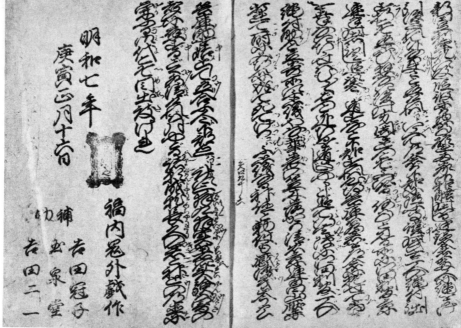

**86.** *Pages from original text of* The Ghost at the Yaguchi Ferry Crossing

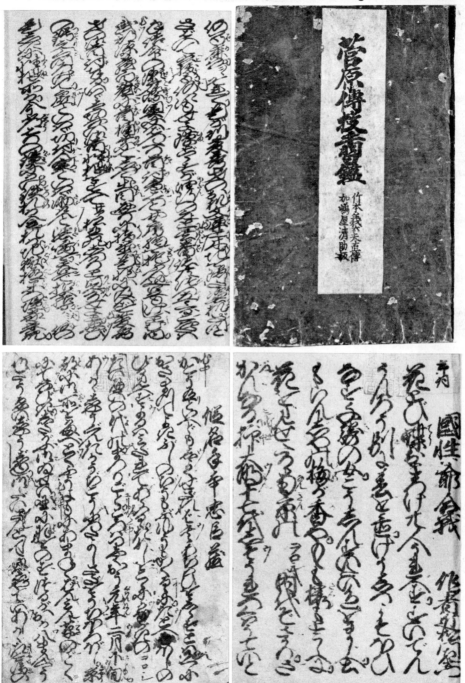

**87.** *Cover and specimen page from original text of* The Tale of Sugawara Michizane

**88.** *Page from original text of* The Faithful Forty-seven

**89.** *Page from original text of* The Battle of Kokusenya

90. Woodblock print: Saruwaka-machi theater district in Edo

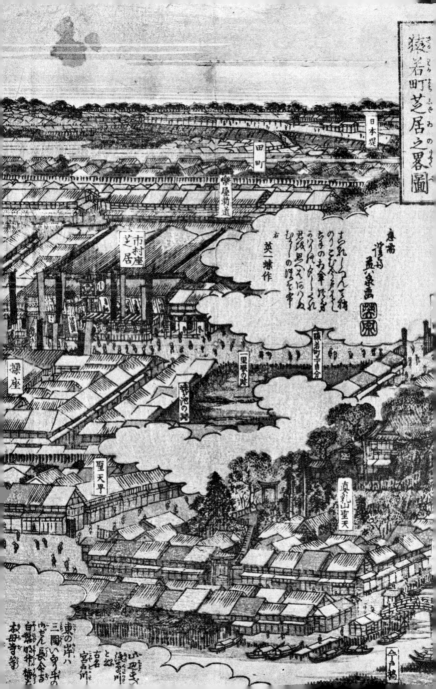

*91. Woodblock print: puppet joruri performance in the late Edo period*

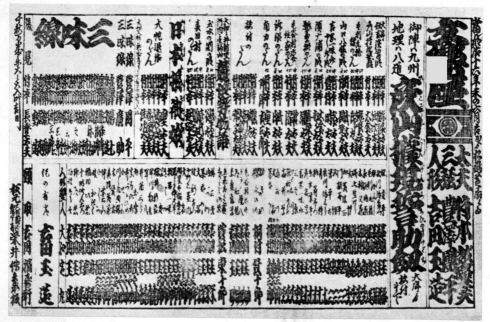

*92. Bunraku program of the Mejii era*

CHAPTER 6

# The Continuation
# of the Line

CHIKUGO-NO-JO LEFT BEHIND a brilliant array of successors to his art. His immediate follower, Gidayu II (1691–1744), became a student of Chikugo-no-jo when he was very young and showed promise from his first lesson. Even so, Chikugo-no-jo continued to refuse to let him appear on the stage, with the result that he finally lost patience, joined the Toyotake-za, and performed there for a time under the name Wakatake Masadayu. The Toyotake-za, which had opened in 1703 and also presented Gidayu-bushi, was the main rival of the Takemoto-za. Since the Toyotake-za was located to the east of Dotombori and the Takemoto-za to the west of it, the brilliant style of the former was referred to as the "east style," while the more subtle style of the latter was called the "west style."

Masadayu returned to the Takemoto-za in 1712 and performed one of the main scenes in *Yosaku of Tamba* (Tamba no Yosaku). In 1714, after Chikugo-no-jo's death, he was chosen by Chikamatsu and Izumo as chief performer of the Takemoto-za and changed his name to Takemoto Masadayu in celebration of this appointment. He continued to improve his art under the guidance of Takemoto Seibo and Ridayu, older students of Chikugo-no-jo, and the next year gained great popularity through his performance of the main scene in Chikamatsu's *Battle of Kokusenya,* setting a new long-run record of seventeen months.

Chikugo-no-jo had established a fashion with his strong, clear voice. By contrast, Masadayu's voice was rather weak, but he made up for it in the introspective weight and strength of his interpretation. He utilized the highest tones of the *shamisen* for his accompaniment and revised many of the old melodies to fit his own voice. He was particularly famous for his interpretation of Chikamatsu's double-suicide plays.

In 1734 Masadayu took the name Gidayu II and in the following year was recognized by the emperor and awarded the imposing name Takemoto Kazusa-no-shojo Fujiwara Yoshinori. The following emperor similarly honored him with a new name, Takemoto Harima-no-shojo II, upon viewing his performance in Chikamatsu's play, *The Night Attack at the Horikawa Mansion During Cherry Blossom Time at the Imperial Palace* (Gosho-zakura Horikawa Youchi).

Toyotake Echizen-no-shojo (1681–1764), who founded the Toyotake-za in 1703, had been one of the oldest students of Chikugo-no-jo and had opened this new theater under the name of Toyotake Wakadayu. Because the theater failed to prosper, he closed it and undertook to tour the provinces for a time. Later he rejoined Chikugo-no-jo at the Takemoto-za. In 1706, with the puppeteer Tatsumatsu Hachirobei as partner, he reopened the Toyotake-za and hired Ki no Kaion(1663–1742) as playwright. In 1718 the emperor awarded him the name of Kozuke-no-shojo Fujiwara Shigekatsu. Under this new title he continued his work as both chief performer and manager of the Toyotake-za. His great success in 1726 with *The Tale of Hojo Tokiyori* (Hojo Tokiyori Ki), a joint work by Nishizawa Ippu and Namiki Sosuke, finally set the Toyotake-za on a solid financial footing. He was recognized once again by the emperor in

1731, at which time he received the name Echizen-no-shojo Fujiwara Shigeyasu. In 1746, at the age of sixty-five, he once more performed *The Tale of Hojo Tokiyori* and then retired from the stage to spend the rest of his life as manager of the theater.

Echizen-no-shojo was the originator of the "west style," for which the Toyotake-za was famous. He was gifted with a beautiful voice, and he used it to the best possible advantage in his brilliant, clear style of Gidayu-bushi. Indeed, Gidayu-bushi was blessed in having such superlative performers as this— men who in their turn trained able successors. In this way the line has continued, and the high artistic level of the art has been preserved to the present day.

# CHAPTER 7

# The Playwright Chikamatsu

THE SUCCESS OF Gidayu-bushi depended to a large extent upon the competence and artistic taste of the narrators, their *shamisen* accompanists, and the puppeteers—and upon their ability to work together—but the creators of the works they performed must not be forgotten. The most successful of these was Chikamatsu Monzaemon (1653–1724).

Chikamatsu was the second son of Sugimori, a member of the Echizen clan. In 1675 he became playwright for Uji Kaga-no-jo's troupe at Shijo in Kyoto. Later, as we have already noted, he was appointed main playwright for Gidayu's troupe in Osaka. He also wrote many plays for the famous Osaka Kabuki actor Sakata Tojuro I. Most celebrated among his works are the double-suicide pieces (*shinju-mono*), which exerted a great influence on Japanese drama in general.

Chikamatsu's achievements were many, but possibly the most important of them was the creation of a five-act dramatic form which in later years became the standard for both Gidayu-bushi and Kabuki. The oldest *ko-joruri* play was *The Twelve-Step Book* (Junidan Soshi), which had set the precedent for twelve acts. But this form was very cumbersome, and the technical and dramatic advances that had been made by the time Chikamatsu arrived on the scene demanded a stronger dramatic structure.

Chikamatsu's new five-act form for period pieces (*jidai-mono*) allowed for the logical spacing out of the basic dramatic struc-

126

ture of introduction, development, and climax. Each act also has the same type of development, with three parts called *kuchi, naka,* and *kiri.* As we have observed before, the *kiri* is even to this day considered the most important and difficult part of each act and is always performed by an experienced narrator.

The first act of a five-act play always opens in a formal or ceremonial setting such as a palace or the front of a temple or a shrine—a setting which lends weight to the piece. The act introduces the characters of the play, usually deals with some incident in the life of the villain, and almost always ends with the hero's being chased off by the villain, who is followed by someone who is going to help the hero win. Thus the viewer is led on a merry chase into the rest of the story.

The second act is not particularly important or interesting. Its basic purpose is to give more details about the situation.

The third act is such an important part of a play that during the middle and later part of the Edo period, when plays were written by groups of writers, the most skillful and famous one among the group was always chosen to write the third act. It contains the action—the most important part of the development of the story.

The fourth act always begins with a *michiyuki* (literally, "road-going"). This is the most poetic and dancelike scene of the play. It shows the characters of the play on their way to some important destination which in some way or other always means an important change in their lives. It tells in almost sung narration and beautiful dancelike movement of the thoughts, reminiscences, hopes, and fears of the person or persons traveling. The scenery always depicts some beautiful stretch of forest, mountain, or seashore and is always set in the season most appropriate to the mood of the traveler or travelers. This fourth act provides artistic beauty and a relaxed atmosphere after the violent action and tension of the third act.

The fifth act brings the play to an end, always with utter defeat for the villain and glorious triumph for the hero.

This form of dramaturgy is in evidence throughout the history of *joruri* and Kabuki after Chikamatsu. Actual division of the acts and scenes is sometimes different, but the basic structure never changes.

In addition to the five-act system for period and historical pieces, Chikamatsu developed a three-act system for plays concerning contemporary life (*sewa-mono*)—a system based on the Noh dramaturgy of Zeami called *jo-ha-kyu* (introduction, development, climax). The *jo* section or first act is an easy, gentle introduction; the *ha* section or second act is the development section, which is full of delicate and detailed rhythms at a faster tempo; and the *kyu* section or third act climaxes and ends the piece in a brilliant *presto* tempo. This technique originated in Gagaku, an ancient form of court music.

Chikamatsu used the *jo-ha-kyu* structure in his *sewa-mono,* the most famous of which are his double-suicide pieces, not only for the overall composition but within each act as well. Thus he was able to reach great heights of poetic beauty and to develop an almost musical overall rhythm. This structure is so important to all classical Japanese dramaturgy and performance techniques that without a feeling for it a play or a performance is very flat and uninteresting.

The two forms of dramaturgy developed by Chikamatsu brought about a radical change in the history of Japanese drama which is felt to this day.

Chikamatsu was also particularly good at characterization. His characters run the whole gamut from peasant to priest to aristocrat, and he covered every period of history from the prehistoric legendary age of the gods right up through to his own day. His sense of period and his understanding of humanity were so superior that all of Japanese history and its various heroes and villains, as well as all those in between, live even for us today.

The skill and beauty of Chikamatsu's language is beyond compare. His great love for and understanding of human beings lends a natural, settled atmosphere to his works. His clean, clear view of history enabled him to write with ease of expression no matter which period he chose. Especially in his contemporary *sewa-mono* pieces, his portrayal of customs and the social atmosphere was always sensitive and correct. Again, he was always on the side of the underdog.

Chikamatsu died at the age of seventy-one in November 1724, ten years after Gidayu I (Chikugo-no-jo). Today, some two and a half centuries later, his plays are a living legacy both in Bunraku and in Kabuki.

CHAPTER 8

# The People of the Takemoto-za and the Toyotake-za

THE TAKEMOTO-ZA, where Gidayu-bushi was born and developed, was located in Dotombori on the site of the present Naniwa-za. From the time when Gidayu I opened it in 1684 until it closed in 1767, the Takemoto-za was the center of the world of puppet *joruri*.

After the death of Gidayu I, when Masadayu (Gidayu II) became head performer at the Takemoto-za, many of the artists moved to the Toyotake-za, but after Masadayu's great success with *The Battle of Kokusenya* the Takemoto-za maintained a solid position until the death of Chikamatsu in 1724. Among Chikamatsu's successors as playwrights for this theater were Bunkodo, Matsuda Wakichi, and Hasegawa Senshi. The puppeteer Yoshida Bunzaburo I (?–1760) matured about this time and became particularly famous for the handling of male puppets. After the death of Masadayu the impresario Takeda Izumo hired the playwright Namiki Sosuke (who later changed his name to Senryu) and thereby once more added strength to the superior position of the Takemoto-za.

Namiki Senryu produced successful plays one after another in collaboration with Takeda Izumo and Miyoshi Shoraku. These works include *The Tale of the Summer Festival in Osaka* (Natsu Matsuri Naniwa Kagami) and *The Tale of Sugawara*

130

*Michizane* (Sugawara Denju Tenarai Kagami). When Takeda Izumo died in 1747, his son Ko-izumo took the name of Izumo II and collaborated with Namiki and Miyoshi in the writing of *Yoshitsune and the Thousand Cherry Trees* (Yoshitsune Sembon-zakura), *The Faithful Forty-seven* (Kanadehon Chushingura), *The Diary Concerning Two Butterflies in the Gay Quarters* (Futatsu Chocho Kuruwa no Nikki), and other plays. Thus, in the Namiki-Miyoshi-Takeda trio of playwrights, the collaborator named Takeda was Takeda Izumo I up to 1746, when *The Tale of Sugawara Michizane* was produced, but in all plays after that date, beginning with *Yoshitsune and the Thousand Cherry Trees*, the name Takeda denotes Takeda Izumo II.

During this period, Gidayu-bushi reached the height of its prosperity and at the same time attained a high level of development in each phase of the art. The result was a healthy competition among narrators, puppeteers, and playwrights.

Twenty-four years after the death of Gidayu II, with the presentation of *The Faithful Forty-seven*, there occurred an event which was unprecedented in the history of puppet joruri. The main performer of the Takemoto-za at that time was Takemoto Konodayu (1700–1768). Konodayu had an especially low voice, which he employed to develop an extremely gorgeous and brilliant style of narration. He was later recognized by the emperor and received the name Toyotake Chikuzen-no-shojo.

On the first day of performance of *The Faithful Forty-seven*, the puppeteer Yoshida Bunzaburo I requested that Konodayu narrate a little more slowly in one particular scene in order to facilitate the movement of the puppets. Konodayu indignantly refused, saying that if the request had been made during rehearsal it would be feasible, but now that the play had already opened, nothing could possibly be changed in any way. Moreover, he said, such a request was an insult to the art of Gidayu-bushi. A heated discussion was still going on between Konodayu and Bunzaburo long after the curtain was supposed to have risen on the first performance. Bunzaburo's request, the ensuing altercation, and the delay were all unheard of in the history of Gidayu-bushi. Somehow, things were smoothed over for the time being, and the play was able to get under way.

Yoshida Bunzaburo had been trained in the puppeteer's art since childhood by his father, Takemoto Saburobei. He was highly talented—to the extent, in fact, that he even directed some of the plays at the Takemoto-za. All puppeteers before his time had specialized in either male or female puppets, but Bunzaburo was expert with any and all puppets. His direction of plays stressed realism to the point of using real water and mud in the murder scene of *The Tale of the Summer Festival at Osaka*, and his interpretation of the part of Yuranosuke in *The Faithful Forty-seven* was so famous that his family crest is used to this day on the costume of Yuranosuke in both Bunraku and Kabuki.

Bunzaburo left the Takemoto-za many times and tried to set up a troupe of his own, but each time he failed and ended up by returning to the fold. In spite of his defections he was welcomed back, for the impresario Izumo respected his talent and, in fact, took sides with him in the quarrel with Konodayu.

In 1734, in the production of *The Tale of Ashiya Doman Ouchi*, Bunzaburo came up with the idea of using three puppeteers to manipulate one puppet. Up to this time, each puppet had been handled by one man only. Bunzaburo's innovation was so successful that it was adopted and has been handed down to the present, creating the form we know today as Bunraku. Of course it made the handling of puppets much more complicated and difficult, but at the same time it broadened the range of expression. It was a revolution that brought Japanese puppet art to a level found nowhere else in the world.

As a result of the disagreement between Konodayu and Bunzaburo, in which Izumo took sides with Bunzaburo, Konodayu left the Takemoto-za and joined the Toyotake-za. He was accompanied in this exodus by several other narrators who also felt that their art itself had been insulted. From this time on, the moving back and forth of various performers between the two theaters became common. Thus the "west style" and the "east style" became one, and the art continued to develop in a single flow. About the same time, however, Kabuki regained its popularity, with the result that both the Takemoto-za and the Toyotake-za went into a financial decline.

After the death of Izumo II in 1756, Izumo III took over his position at the Takemoto-za. At about the same time the theater acquired as its playwright the last great writer for the puppet stage, Chikamatsu Hanji (1725–83), who gained fame with such plays as *Proper Upbringing of a Young Lady at Mount Imose* (Imose-yama Onna Teikin) and *The New Ballad Singer* (Shimpan Utazaimon). But the days of the Takemoto-za as a puppet theater were numbered, and its last production, a Chikamatsu Hanji play, was presented in December 1767. From that time on, it served as a Kabuki theater.

The Toyotake-za had opened its doors for the first time in 1703, but it gained its first real recognition in 1726 with its production of *The Tale of Hojo Tokiyori,* which ran for ten months. After this success it continued to develop its own style with a troupe centered around Chikuzen-no-shojo as its chief performer. New plays produced during the following years included Kaion's *Red Cherry Blossoms and the Love of Oshichi the Grocer's Daughter* (Yaoya Oshichi Koi no Hi-zakura) and Sosuke's

*Tale of Yoichi of Nasu and the Western Sea* (Nasu no Yoichi Seikai Suzuri).

Among the narrators, Komadayu (?–1777) was famous for his brilliant performance of the main scenes in *The Chronicle of the Battle of Ichinotani* (Ichinotani Futaba Gunki) and *The Tale of the Believers at the Gion Festival* (Gion Sairei Shinko Ki). His style was characterized by his high voice, which he used particularly well in showing the differences in social status among the various characters.

The main puppeteer at the Toyotake-za was Fujii Kohachiro, who was especially skillful in handling female puppets. In later years he worked in Edo (present Tokyo), but even though he was well known in his time, we do not know the dates of his birth and death. Another puppeteer in the same troupe was Fujii Kosaburo, who was also famous for his handling of female puppets. He made many improvements on the one-man puppets before the system of three men to one puppet was introduced.

After Konodayu joined the Toyotake-za as a result of his dispute with Bunzaburo, this theater enjoyed a short period of greater popularity than the Takemoto-za. Unfortunately, however, in the following years the constant exchange of personnel between the two theaters destroyed the competitive spirit, and the art went into a period of decline. In 1765 the Toyotake-za ended its career, and two years later, as we have seen, the Takemoto-za was forced to follow suit.

In later years many plays were written, but hardly a one of them is worth mentioning. At the same time, however, there were important developments in the construction and handling of the puppets. The puppeteer Wakatake Tokuro (dates of birth and death unknown), who later took the name Tekkyu, made many improvements in puppet technique and was second

only to Bunzaburo I in this respect. It was Tokuro who invented
puppets with movable eyebrows and movable fingers.

Movable eyebrows added to the range of facial expression,
and movable fingers, which are made by fastening the joints
together with strips of leather, allowed a much wider range of
movement. Tokuro was particularly famous for his handling of
male puppets, and it is in these puppets that his innovations
are mainly used. His performance of such characters as Kagekiyo and Kumagai received especially high praise.

Among narrators of the late Edo period, Kanedayu (1730–
79) was celebrated for his strong, beautiful voice and his wide
range. Another narrator of the time, Fumotodayu (1730–1822),
was an amateur who offered his services at a time of crisis in the
Toyotake-za. His real name was Nabeso of Semba, and he chose
the stage name Fumotodayu ( *fumoto* means "foothills") as an
indication of modesty when he appeared alongside professionals
in higher positions than his own. Echizen-no-shojo, the head
of the troupe at the Toyotake-za, died in 1764, and in the following year the theater closed its doors—two years before the
Takemoto-za gave its last performance and was converted into
a Kabuki theater.

# CHAPTER 9

# The Bunraku-za
# of the Meiji Period and After

SOMETIME BETWEEN 1789 and 1800, Uemura Bunrakuken (1737–1810) came to Osaka from Awaji Island and in 1805 formed a troupe of Gidayu-bushi players. The troupe was successful, but it had no permanent home. In 1811, the year after Bunrakuken's death, it settled in a theater on the grounds of the Naniwa Shrine in Bakuro-machi, Osaka. Many years of alternating hardship and success lay ahead, and time was to bring inevitable changes in its membership, but the organization survived. In 1871 it established itself in Matsushima, another part of Osaka, and performed there under the name Bunraku-za.

In 1884, when a rival troupe called the Hikoroku-za invaded the Bunraku-za's territory and began to perform near the north gate of the Inari Shrine in Dotombori, the Bunraku-za bought a theater on the grounds of the Goryo Shrine.

In 1889, when Taizo VI took over as head of the troupe, it was more successful than it had ever been before, but in 1909, having encountered financial difficulties, it came under the management of the Shochiku company, which controlled a wide sector of the Japanese theatrical world. At that time the troupe consisted of thirty-eight narrators, fifty-one *shamisen* players, and twenty-four puppeteers.

136

In 1926 a fire completely destroyed the Goryo Bunraku-za and brought its forty-five-year history to an end. After this calamity the troupe performed for a time at the Benten-za in Dotombori. During the following year it bought the Chika-matsu-za at Yotsuhashi, in Osaka, renovated it, changed its name to the Bunraku-za, and once more set up a permanent home. The new theater, with its excellent facilities and its seating capacity of 850, was ideal for the presentation of the art that had now come to be known as Bunraku.

During the Pacific War the Bunraku-za was used as a movie theater. After the war it was the first legitimate theater to resume business, presenting its initial postwar performance in February 1946. In 1949 a number of the narrators, *shamisen* players, and puppeteers formed a labor union, and the Bunraku-za split into rival factions over disagreements regarding the policies of the Shochiku Company, producing two groups called the Mitsuwa-kai and the Chinami-kai. The Mitsuwa-kai broke away from the Shochiku Company in 1950 and set itself up as an itinerant troupe, giving performances in Tokyo, Osaka, and the provinces.

In 1956 the Shochiku Company built a new theater in Do-tombori, naming it the Bunraku-za. In November of the same year the Mitsuwa-kai and the Chinami-kai were once more brought together in a performance sponsored by the Ministry of Education at the Shimbashi Embujo in Tokyo. Seven years later, in 1963, the Bunraku Association was formed, bringing all performers back together. This organization has been charged with the management of all phases of the art since that time.

Also in 1963 the old Bunraku-za in Dotombori, which was still owned by the Shochiku Company, was renovated and given the name of Asahi-za. Even though Bunraku itself is now completely independent of Shochiku's control, all Osaka performances are still held at the Shochiku-owned Asahi-za.

Until the advent of the Bunraku Association, Tokyo performances were held at the Shimbashi Embujo by the Chinami-kai and at the Mitsukoshi Theater by the Mitsuwa-kai. After the opening of the National Theater in November 1966, its small hall became the Tokyo home of Bunraku, which is performed there four months out of every year.

93. *Narrator Takemoto Koshijidayu IV and* shamisen *player Nozawa Kizaemon II*

**94.** *Acting area of Bunraku stage*

95. *Puppet heads at National Theater, Tokyo*

96. *Preparation of a puppet head for a performance*

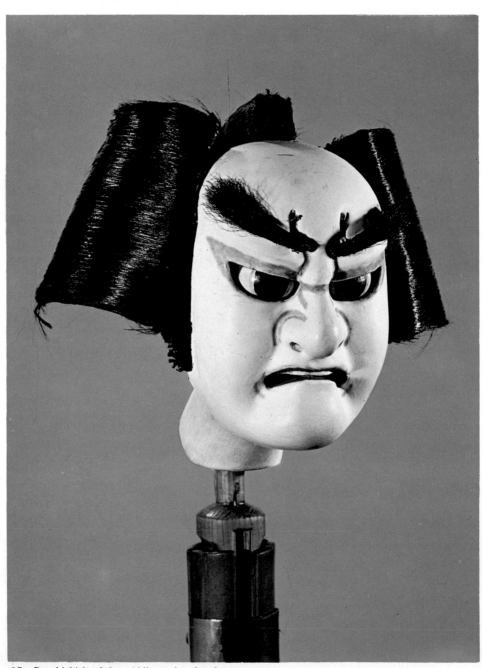

97. *Bunshichi head for middle-aged male roles*

98. *Musume head for young female roles*

99. *Puppets in dressing room before a performance*

# CHAPTER 10

# Bunraku Artists
# of Late Edo and Meiji

TAKEMOTO NAGATODAYU III (1800–1864) was often referred to as
the greatest narrator since Gidayu I. He was a master of all
phases of the art and could hold an audience spellbound in any
scene, from the most formal to the most sentimental. His accompanist, Toyozawa Dampei II, who began his career by join-
ing Nagatodayu at the age of twenty-seven, became the most
celebrated *shamisen* player of the Meiji era.

Since very few new plays of any value were being written, the
art of Bunraku continued to develop by polishing its repertoire
of classical masterpieces. Efforts were made to revive the styles
of the old Takemoto-za and Toyotake-za and to present each
play in the style of the narrator who had originally performed it.
Nagatodayu III was responsible for standardizing the repertoire, making the differences in style and technique clear, and
passing the established techniques on to the next generation.

The first professional narrator from Edo was Tsunadayu VI,
who studied with Nagatodayu III and won fame with his beautiful voice. Another of Nagatodayu's students, Yadayu V, was
celebrated for his sharply cynical interpretations.

Takemoto Harudayu V (1808–77) was the son of a blacksmith. (We may recall here that the great Gidayu I was the son of
a farmer and at the same time note that Bunraku made no

147

social distinctions in its choice of talent.) Like Tsunadayu VI, Harudayu was renowned for his beautiful voice. He was also widely known for his broad-minded interpretations.

Somedayu VI (1797–1869) ranked with Nagatodayu III and Harudayu V as one of the three leading narrators of the late Edo period. He was particularly effective in his third-act performances in historical dramas. His diary is one of the most valuable treatises on Bunraku in existence today.

The style of Koutsubodayu I (1827–78) was strictly in the classical tradition. He was especially adept at moving his audiences to tears in scenes of tragedy and deep sorrow. There was something ironically appropriate in this ability of his, for in February 1878 he was stabbed to death in a quarrel with a stagehand. It is said that his influence in maintaining the strict classical traditions was so great that, had he lived longer, the art of Bunraku would probably be quite different from what it is today.

Another artist of note during late Edo and early Meiji was the blind narrator Sumidayu IV (1829–89). Before the opening day of each performance Sumidayu reviewed and perfectly memorized the complicated librettos by having one of his students read the whole play to him three times. He was noted for his fine voice and for his carefully studied interpretations of *sewamono* plays. In one instance, in preparation for narrating a certain play, he rode all the way to the distant Sumiyoshi Shrine in a rickshaw in order to learn the exact breathing rhythms of a rickshaw man.

Takemoto Settsu-no-taisho (1836–1917) began his youthful training as a *shamisen* player. Later, however, because he was gifted with an excellent voice, he became a narrator. He studied under Harudayu V and, at the age of forty-seven, was promoted to the position of main performer for the troupe, succeeding the deceased Koutsubodayu. Soon after his promotion he took the name Harudayu VI. In 1913 the emperor awarded him the title Settsu-no-taisho, and during the same year he retired. His dignified style, his superb voice, and his phenomenal breath control made him one of the most memorable of narrators. His most famous interpretation was that of the role of Princess Yaegaki in *Twenty-four Expressions of Filial Love* (Honcho Nijushiko).

Like his teacher Harudayu V, Osumidayu III was the son of a blacksmith. He took the name Osumidayu when he joined the Hikoroku-za along with his *shamisen* player Dampei II after a disagreement at the Bunraku-za. Although he never found it convenient to settle down in any one place for long, he was very strict in maintaining high standards of performance, both for himself and for those with whom he worked.

Even though Osumidayu and Settsu-no-taisho had been trained by the same teacher, their styles were as different as night and day. The contrast between Settsu-no-taisho's refined, dignified, romantic style and Osumidayu's strong, moving, realistic style made the Meiji era a colorful one in the history of Bunraku.

Among the outstanding puppeteers of the time was Yoshida Tamazo I (1829–1905), who later changed his name to Oyatama I. He was a contemporary of the *shamisen* player Dampei II. His son Tamazo II was extremely skillful at interpreting "soft" roles like those of princesses and wealthy young men, but unfortunately he died quite young—long before his father. In 1872, in the advertisements posted outside the theater, the name of Oyatama I appeared in the same size of characters as that of Harudayu V, marking the first time in Bunraku history that a puppeteer held a position in a troupe equal to that of the chief narrator.

Oyatama was famous for his handling of the puppets for such roles as those of rough men, clowns, and animals and was particularly fond of spectacular tricks, including quick changes in view of the audience and stunts in which both he and the puppets were made to fly through the air suspended from wires. He was numbered among the three top performers of his time, first with Nagatodayu III and Dampei II and then, after the death of the former, with Dampei and Settsu-no-taisho.

Oyatama's son-in-law, Kiritake Monjuro I (1847?–1910), spent his younger days studying and training in Edo, but around the beginning of the Meiji era he returned to the Bunraku-za. From that time on, he worked closely with Oyatama and became highly skilled in the handling of female puppets. He is still remembered as one of the most important figures in the Bunraku world of Meiji times.

Yoshida Taizo (1864–1916?) also deserves mention as an outstanding Meiji puppeteer. His art was more subtle than that of most puppeteers, and he was therefore not as popular with the public as others, but his highly developed technique was greatly respected by those who knew the art well. We are told that Taizo often lent his cap to his student Eiza and allowed him to perform as the main puppeteer, while Taizo himself replaced Eiza as operator of the puppet's left hand. The purpose of this change of places, of course, was to help Eiza learn the art and give him more concrete experience. The puppeteer's cap, which also covers his face, is the only means by which the audience can tell who is serving as main puppeteer during a performance. Each puppeteer expresses his individuality by some small difference in the shape of the cap or his method of wearing it. It was thus the mark of his own individuality that Taizo lent to his student, thereby expressing his desire to pass on the art to the new generation as quickly and completely as possible. The act was unprecedented in the history of Bunraku, and it is gratifying to know that Eiza, as a result of Taizo's dedicated teaching, became the most skilled puppeteer of his troupe—a position which he held throughout the Taisho era (1912–26) and well into the present Showa era.

# CHAPTER 11

# Recent and Present Artists

IT IS NOW MORE THAN forty years that I have been closely associated with Bunraku. In 1926, when this association began, the main narrator was Tsudayu III. Two other famous narrators of that day were Tosadayu VI and Koutsubodayu II. Each of these three had his own distinctive style, and together they represented the full range of the traditions that make up the art of Gidayu-bushi. Of the first two, I shall speak briefly here; of the third, I shall have more to say later on.

Tsudayu III (1869–1941) became the main performer in 1924. His was a magnificent and heroic style in which the old Gidayu-bushi traditions and flavor were maintained. Tosadayu VI (1863–1941) spent his younger days studying under the Tosa clansman and Meiji political leader Goto Shojiro but later entered the Bunraku world to study under Osumidayu III and finally under Settsu-no-taisho. His voice had a tendency to waver at times, but his interpretations were sensitive and emotional, and he had the power to enrapture an audience. His favorite scene—and consequently the one he was most famous for—was the Wineshop (Sakaya) scene in *The Woman in a Gaudy Dance Costume* (Hadesugata Onna Maiginu), the play about the star-crossed lovers Osono and Hanshichi. In fact, he was so celebrated for his performance of this scene that it was presented literally every time he appeared in Tokyo.

In Gidayu-bushi each scene has been handed down in the

152

style of the narrator who first performed it or who perfected it, and thus the art retains its original flavor to a greater degree than most of the traditional performing arts do. Why does Bunraku have a stricter and more stable set of traditions than Kabuki, the classical dance, and *shamisen* music? One of the chief reasons is that during the Meiji era the introduction of foreign culture greatly influenced all the traditional arts except Bunraku. The narrators have always handed down their art regardless of the changes in the world around them. On the other hand, Kabuki (to give one example) allowed itself to be penetrated by new influences and, as a result, suffers from the effects of these influences today. In other words, it is no longer a traditional art in pure form. The art of Bunraku, however, had no cracks through which such influences could enter. Thus it has maintained its position as the purest and most resistant—indeed most stubborn—of the traditional performing arts of Japan.

Bunraku has been able to maintain its fine old traditions even though—or perhaps because—it is unhampered by the headmaster (*iemoto*) system common to all other traditional Japanese arts. In fact, if we look for anything in Bunraku resembling the headmasters in other arts, we find only the narrators who first performed or perfected each act and scene, since it was these men, long dead and gone, whose interpretations were to be meticulously handed down as yardsticks for the performances we see today. The resemblance, however, is slight, and Bunraku has never really had any headmasters in the ordinary sense of the word.

Throughout the long history of the art, the narrators of Bunraku have almost always been men born and bred in Osaka. A notable exception was Toyotake Koutsubodayu II (1878–1967), who was born and raised in Tokyo and became the main performer of the Bunraku-za. He was awarded numerous honors, including nomination to the National Academy of Art in 1946 and, in 1947, recognition by the household of Prince Chichibu, which granted him the name Yamashiro-no-shojo. (It is this name by which he is remembered today.) He retired from the stage in 1959, and in 1960 he was named by the government as a "person of cultural merit."

Yamashiro-no-shojo's style was dignified, fresh, and clear. He was particularly skillful at setting the mood of the natural scenery of a play. In fact, he even spoke of his likes and dislikes among various plays and scenes in terms of the natural settings they employed.

He was an avid collector of books and documents concerning Bunraku and was especially interested in old librettos, which he used for restoring many details of dialogue which had been neglected or lost through the years. This interest of his greatly influenced his own performances and heightened their interest. More than that, however, it was an invaluable contribution to the art of Bunraku as a whole.

The first time I attended a performance by Yamashiro-no-shojo (at that time he still went by the name of Koutsubodayu II), I felt as though I were hearing Gidayu-bushi for the first time. After that, I experienced the same feeling every time I attended one of his performances. It was his fresh and vivid style of presentation that gave me this sensation of newness.

My own father was a Gidayu-bushi narrator, and Gidayu-bushi was very much a part of my life from the time I was born. Even so, Yamashiro-no-shojo's performances never ceased to surprise me with their freshness and vigor—to the point, in fact, that I often thought I was hearing a piece I had never heard before. The only other artist who ever provided me with this

100. *Entrance to National Theater, Tokyo*

101. *Interior of small hall, National Theater, Tokyo, during a Bunraku performance*

102. *Puppeteer waiting for entrance cue*

103. Tozai *announcement at beginning of a performance*

104. *Stage viewed from wings*

105. *Puppeteers during a performance*

106. *Performance viewed from wings*

107. *Sceneshifter awaiting his cue*

*108.* Kakeai: *the use of numerous narrators and* shamisen *players in one play*

*109. View of stage from above during a performance*

*110–13 (top row). The narrator Tsunadayu VIII*

*114–15 (bottom row). The* shamisen *player Kizaemon II*

116–17.   *Two views of puppeteers' dressing
room, National Theater, Tokyo*

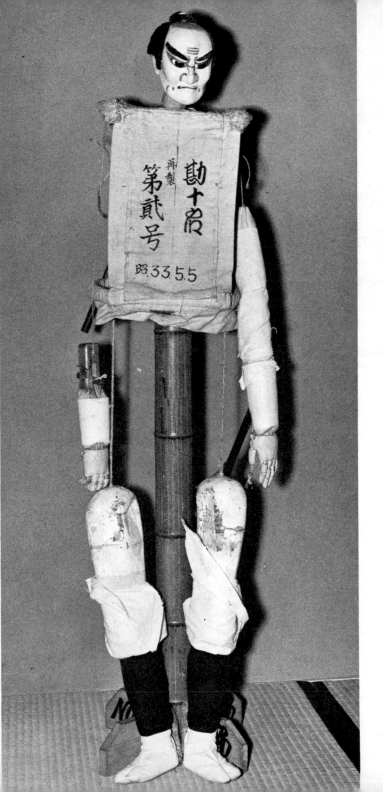

120. *Body and head of male puppet*

121. *Body of female puppet with undercollar in place*

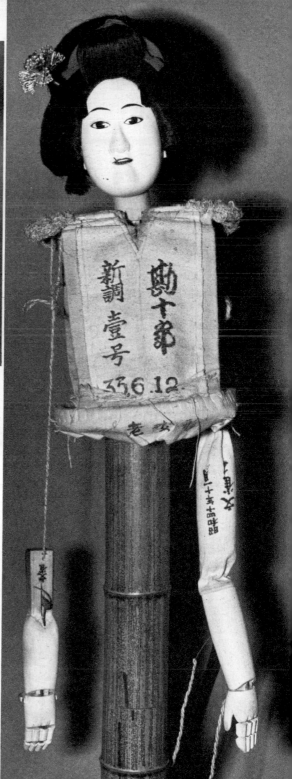

122. *Base and head of female puppet*

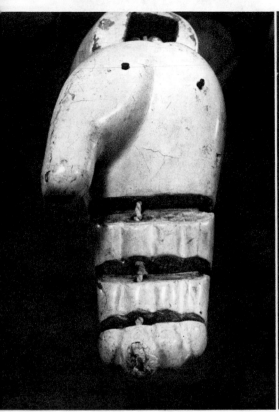

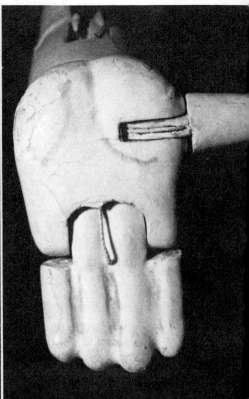

123. *Puppet hand with four fingers movable as single unit*

124. *Puppet hand with movable joints*

127. *Puppet hand designed for holding a fan*

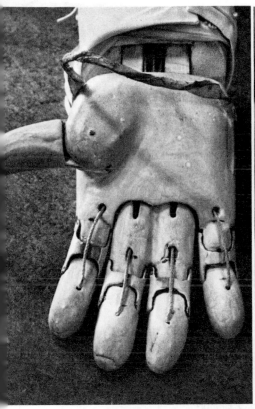

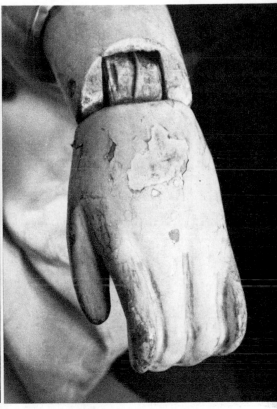

125. *Puppet hand with movable fingers and wrist*

126. *Puppet hand movable only at wrist*

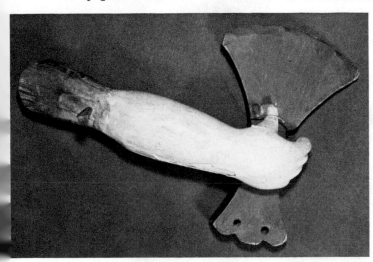

128. *Puppet hand with plectrum for playing Japanese lute*

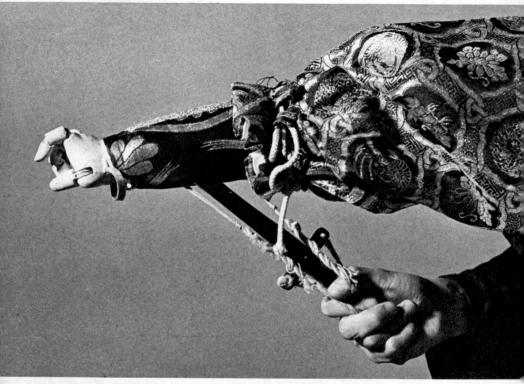

129. *Fully jointed puppet hand closed into a fist*

131–32. *Manipulation of movable eyebrows in male-puppet head*

130. *Fully jointed puppet hand opened wide*

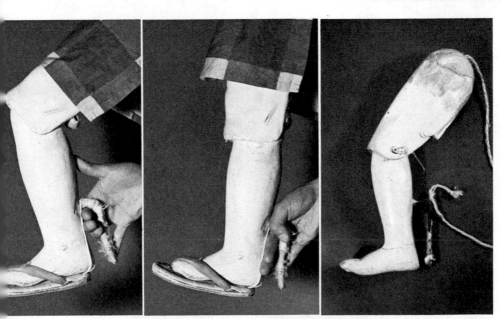

133–35. *Manipulation of male-puppet leg*

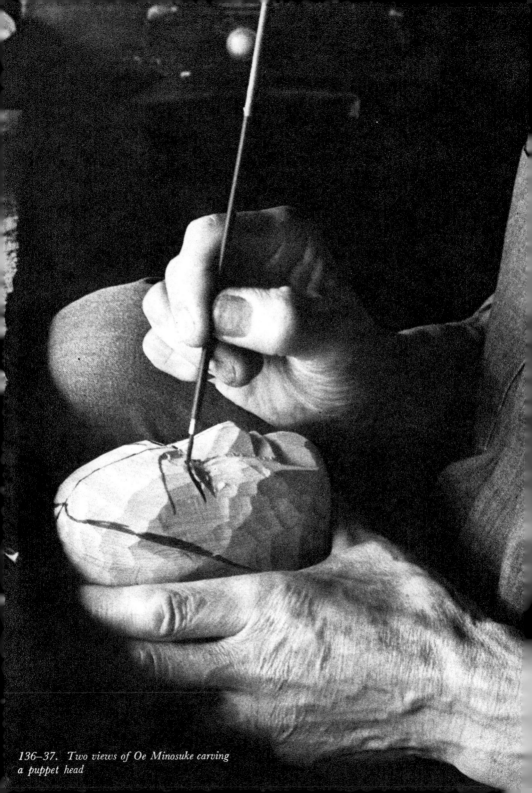

136–37. *Two views of Oe Minosuke carving a puppet head*

140. *Bunshichi head used for middle-aged male roles*

*141.* Waka-otoko *head*

*142.* Genta *head*

*145.* Oniwaka *head*

*146.* Yokambei *head*

143. *Komei head*     144. *Kebiishi head*

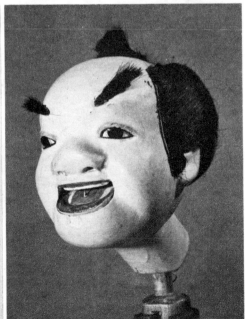

147. *Darasuke head*     148. *Matabei head*

149. *Ojuto head*     150. *Torao head*     151. *Masamune head*

153. *Shiratayu head*

152. *Kiichi head*

154. *Takeuji head*

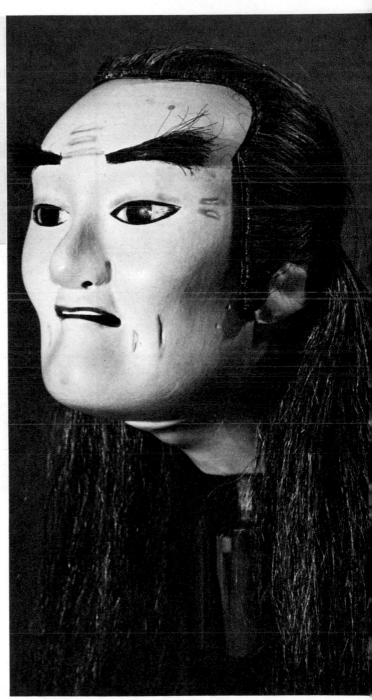

155. *Sadanoshin head*

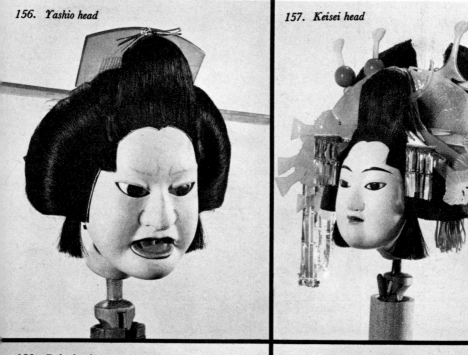

156. *Yashio head*

157. *Keisei head*

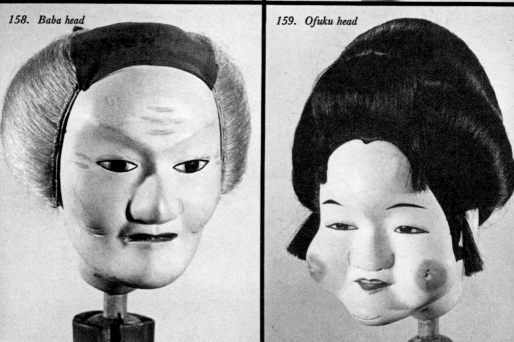

158. *Baba head*

159. *Ofuku head*

*161–62 (above). Gabu head used for roles of
demons disguised as beautiful women*

*163. (opposite page). Kagekiyo head
used only for role of Kagekiyo*

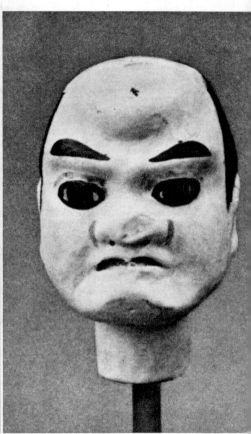

164. *Tsume head used for minor female roles*

165. *Tsume head used for minor male roles*

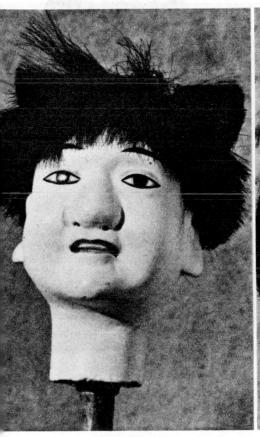 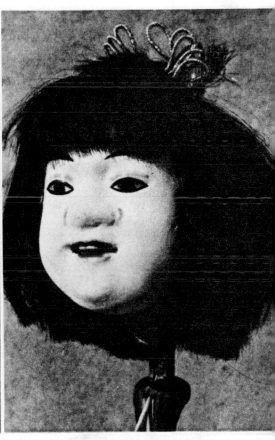

166.   *Koyaku head used for male child roles*

167.   *Koyaku head used for female child roles*

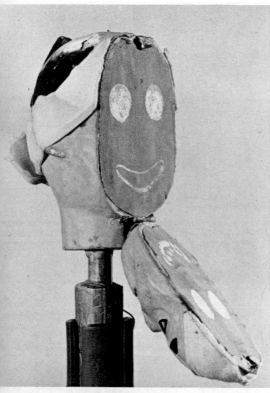

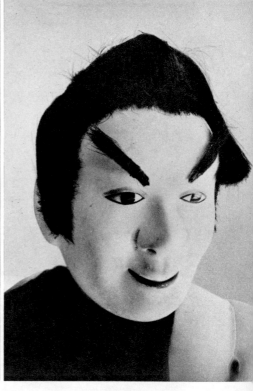

*168–69.  Nashi-wari head used for minor characters in sword fights*

*170.  Chari head used for roles of comic young male servants*

169

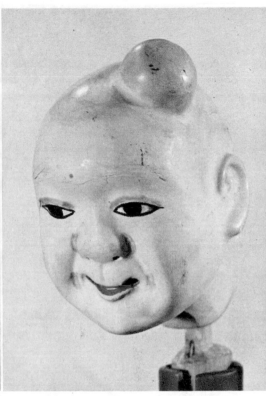

171. *Chari head used for comic male roles*  172. *Myorin head used for comic nun roles*

*173. Asahi-za at Dotombori: Osaka home of Bunraku*

type of experience was the Kabuki actor Onoe Kikugoro VI.

One time I asked Yamashiro-no-shojo about this seeming newness of his interpretations. He was somewhat disturbed, answering that he only strove to perform each piece exactly as it had been passed down to him by his teachers. Such was the vigor and strength of his talent that it broke through and rose above the stereotypes of Bunraku, giving the strict old traditions a new life and energy without the necessity of tricks or innovations. Technically, instead of stressing the beauty of the voice, Yamashiro-no-shojo placed chief emphasis on the quality of the tones and the use of the sounds to produce a deeper, clearer rendering of the mood and the story. This was the basic reason for the freshness and vigor of his performances.

He had the power to set the whole scene in one phrase. His utterance of "The sun has already begun to sink silently in the west" gave one that tense twilight feeling of expectation. When he intoned, "Only the clouded snowy sky . . ." one felt a bleak loneliness and drew one's coat a little tighter in protection against the whistling foreboding winds. His delineation of four or five characters in one scene was sometimes clearer and more accurate than when that same scene is played by as many separate actors in Kabuki. I have never observed the work of a greater genius and master in Bunraku or in any other art.

All the good present-day narrators, including Tsunadayu VIII, Tsudayu IV, Koshijidayu IV, and many others, were either direct or second-generation students of Yamashiro-no-shojo, and they all seem to have received inspiration from his genius. Since those of the younger generation now being trained by these men are showing great promise, there seems to be no fear that the art will die out.

As for the art of the *shamisen*, its richness is quite amazing.

Among the particularly impressive players I have heard, I may mention Matsutaro I, Dohachi I, Tomojiro VI, Senshi V, Kichibei VII, Tsunazo IV, and Seiroku IV—all men who developed their own individual characteristics while upholding the traditions of their predecessors.

At present there are two *shamisen* masters who deserve special mention: Kanji VI and Kizaemon II. They are both highly talented, and their styles are extremely different. Kanji's style, distinguished by his strong, heavy tones, is stirring and heroic. Kizaemon, who plays with a delicately sensitive touch, has a beautiful, rather passionate style which creates an atmosphere of days gone by.

Both of these men might well be called miracle workers in the creation of mood and atmosphere. Kanji was born in 1887 and is the oldest active performer in the world of Bunraku today. Although he is now past eighty, every performance he gives is full of life and artistry. Kizaemon has experienced a succession of illnesses and accidents that would have caused a normal man to give up and retire, but he has never once relaxed his exhausting training schedule and has continued to perform through any and all crises.

The younger generation of *shamisen* players, not to be outdone by the narrators, are also working hard to carry on the traditions of their elders. It is the good fortune of Bunraku to have such diligent prospective successors to its present *shamisen* masters.


I have already spoken of the fine narrator Yamashiro-no-shojo. Indeed, I consider myself very fortunate to have lived during the time when he was active on the stage. There was one other artist who gave me this same feeling of having had immense good luck in enjoying his performances. He was the puppeteer Yoshida Eiza I (1872–1945)—the same Eiza who has been introduced earlier as the favorite student of the Meiji puppeteer Yoshida Taizo.

During his early years Eiza specialized in the handling of female and young male puppets, but around the time that I first saw him perform, in 1927, he became the main puppeteer in the troupe and turned to the handling of warrior and older male puppets. His masterful interpretation of all male roles— from the violent, brash warrior and the dark, shadowy villain to the dreamy lover—was absolutely unforgettable. I shall always remember in particular one time at the Meiji-za, in Tokyo, when Eiza interpreted the role of Kagekiyo in *Hyuga Island*, with Tsudayu III as narrator and, if I recall correctly, Tomojiro VI as *shamisen* player.

Kagekiyo, a former Heike warrior, has almost totally blinded himself and become a recluse on Hyuga Island in mourning for the defeat of the Heike. His daughter Hitomaru, after searching far and wide, finds him there. At first he denies that he is Kagekiyo, but he is finally touched by Hitomaru's longing to see him and talk to him for a short time. After their brief meeting she boards the boat in which she came and sets out for the mainland, leaving behind a letter to her father. Almost sightless, he painfully reads the letter only to discover from it that Hitomaru has sold herself as a prostitute in order to provide him with the money that she has enclosed. Kagekiyo leaps to his feet, waves his arms wildly, and shouts for Hitomaru to come back, but her boat has already gone too far out to sea.

At the moment in the performance when Kagekiyo realizes what has happened and jumps up to beckon with arms spread wide, Tsudayu hit his reading stand with the flat of his hand, giving it a resounding whack, and shot up onto his knees as though he were going to fly right out into the audience. At the same instant, Eiza's Kagekiyo rose up with blinded eyes wide open and arms flung wide. Again, at the same instant, Tomo-jiro's *shamisen* seemed to express the same desperation. The rapport among the three men at this point was an overwhelming experience for all of us in the audience.

I was still a student at that time. My seat was just below the box seats, to the left of the stage. I became so excited that I found, a few seconds later, that I had jumped up and was sitting on top of the back of the seat. Then I heard perfectly timed applause which came from one of the box seats behind me. I myself was so awestruck that I had forgotten to applaud. In fact, I don't think I could have applauded if I had wanted to—I was so overwhelmed by the powerful artistry and timing of the scene.

I was further astonished at the perfect timing and almost artistic quality of the applause I had heard behind me. Turning to see who had expressed his appreciation so effectively, I was hardly surprised to discover that it was the great Kabuki actor Nakamura Kichiemon. I thought to myself that certainly at least this one part of the audience was appropriate to the master-ful performance we had just seen.

Eiza I died late in 1945 in a village in Nara Prefecture where he had taken refuge during the Pacific War. It is sad to think that this superior artist left the scene without ever having be-come a member of the Art Academy. In this sense, he was one of the victims of that unfortunate war, since the honor would certainly have come to him in postwar years.

Eiza's contemporary, Yoshida Bungoro I (1869–1963), sur-vived the war, became a member of the Art Academy, and was awarded the name Naniwa-no-jo by the emperor. Before the war he often performed together with Eiza. He was a strong technician, and his art was brilliant and sensual—a perfect contrast to the subtle, introspective art of Eiza. With Bungoro's appearance the stage always seemed to take on added light and gorgeousness. His technique was so strong that he was able to handle puppets in the roles of beautiful young girls even after he had become quite old. After he had reached middle age, and the war was over, his art became somewhat more like that of his former partner Eiza. Although he still maintained his brilliance of execution, he grew more introspective and concentrated more on expressing the heart of the character he was portraying. This new inner meaning, added to his splendid technique, produced an astounding effect. Bungoro was excellent not only in period pieces and the more realistic *sewa-mono* but also in dance scenes and new plays.

His leading student, Kiritake Monjuro II (1900–), is the most important puppeteer in the world of Bunraku today. Among Monjuro's own students are such promising figures as Kanjuro II, Minosuke III, and Seijuro IV, each of whom is developing a distinctive personal style. The younger generation of puppeteers is progressing more rapidly today because of the scarcity of men in the generation before them—a situation which gives them the chance to perform more frequently.

Another present-day master puppeteer is Yoshida Eiza II (1903–), who handles both male and female puppets with striking effect. His best work is to be seen in the roles of young men in Chikamatsu's double-suicide plays.

Others who deserve mention among today's outstanding puppeteers are Kamematsu IV, who works with both male and female puppets; Tamagoro II, whose interpretations are especially delicate; and Tamao, whose handling of male puppets is strong and heroic. Again, there are Tatsugoro V and Kuni-hide, who are especially good at expressing the subtleties of old-woman roles, and of course the previously mentioned Hyoji, whose *tozai* announcement is without equal. These old-guard artists are invaluable to the existence of Bunraku today—and to the passing on of its traditions to future generations.

# CHAPTER 12

# The Meaning of Tradition

IN DESCRIBING THE ART of Bunraku, I have concentrated on the people in its history, for it is they who constitute its essence and who have passed it on from generation to generation. Bunraku lives in its performers, and without them it would have no existence at all. A tradition, by its very meaning, must be handed down and received. In this process it must also be properly understood and appreciated by each generation.

Bunraku, like any other traditional art, has standards which must be maintained. The upholding of these standards is accomplished first of all by concentrating on transmitting the form of the art according to a strict set of rules rather than by transmitting its content alone. The role of human ethics in the transmission of a traditional art is a most important one. In the case of Bunraku the younger generation has always been eager to receive and carry on the traditions.

The code of ethics represented by the single character *gi*—the *gi* which we have earlier noted as the one used by Gidayu I in his name—is an expression of fine moral truth. This truth has been valid through ages past, is valid today, and will continue to be valid as long as human beings exist in this world. All the high ideals and exalted emotions expressed by Bunraku today, especially in the traditions of Gidayu-bushi, stem directly from the spirit of its founder, Gidayu I.

Throughout the long history of Bunraku, no matter how

skilled and famous a performer may have become, he has always given full credit to his teachers and those who came before him and has always been humble about his own ability. This attitude is not just a pose.

Soon after the war there was a joint performance of *The Faithful Forty-seven* by the Shochiku troupe (Chinami-kai) and the Mitsuwa-kai troupe at the Mitsukoshi Theater in Tokyo. Tsunadayu performed the very difficult Yamashina scene. On opening day he was in perfect form, and his performance was truly masterly. But I heard that when he returned to the dressing room he was in a vicious mood. I asked him about this later, and he explained to me that the Yamashina scene was always performed by the top narrator alive at the time—the man who commanded the greatest authority in the art. Thus the performance of this scene had never been simply a matter of whether or not one could handle it. The tradition had always been for the main performer to refuse when he was first asked by the impresario to perform this scene. Then the impresario would wait a respectable amount of time and make his request again before the narrator would consent to perform it. This is how important the Yamashina scene has always been considered. It is such a difficult piece that if a narrator believed there was someone anywhere in Japan who could perform it with greater skill than he, he would most certainly refuse to perform it in public.

When Tsunadayu performed the Yamashina scene at the Mitsukoshi Theater, he was bothered throughout the performance by the idea that he was not in a position to perform it—that he was only doing it in place of someone else. This was the reason for his vicious temper when he left the stage and entered the dressing room.

The person in whose place he had performed was his teacher Yamashiro-no-shojo, who was at that time living a quiet retired life in Kyoto. In some seventy years of active life on the stage, Yamashiro-no-shojo had never performed this particular scene. This was the reason why Tsunadayu felt so strongly about the inappropriateness of his own performance at that time. In fact, he felt so strongly about it that tears came to his eyes as he explained it to me.

Ever since Japan's defeat in World War II there has been a tendency among the Japanese people to reject those things which have been passed down over the centuries, just because they are old. The belief that "old" meant "bad" became fairly widespread and continues to be strong even today. The feeling is at least partly due to the fact that during the war all things intrinsically Japanese were twisted to fit radically nationalistic ideals and were forced upon the people. A violent postwar reaction to such policies was only natural. Still, even though such a reaction can be cited as one reason for the rejection of old traditions, I believe that the loss of attraction in Japan's traditional arts is more than anything else a result of the lack of true effort by those who practice the arts to give them life and meaning in the present-day world.

True art cannot be passed on as popular songs which can be hummed and sung by the man in the street but must be learned and polished through strict discipline on the part of both the teacher and the student. The idea that seems to be prevalent today is that the traditional arts and their strict discipline are only for stuffy old people and that new arts relevant to the modern age will be born naturally without that sort of unpleasant discipline and training. People who think this way are sadly mistaken.

As a result of this tendency to discard the values and disciplines of the traditional arts and to search ever more frantically for new arts to take their place, both the really old and the really new become increasingly rare, and we are left for the most part with arts that are a hopeless jumble of both. True art, however, allows nothing which is halfway.

The traditional arts must not only be handed down from generation to generation but must also be reinterpreted and repurified by each generation in order that they may communicate with the people of that age. This is what gives traditions their attractiveness and meaningfulness—their life in each new age. It is lack of participation that allows an art to become moldy and old-fashioned—fit only for museums.

Traditions are valuable not because they are old but because they have an element of life, a universal appeal and meaning, which has survived through the ages, having been preserved and repolished by men of talent and insight. It is when these truths are forgotten and the effort to preserve them dies out that traditions become mere conventions—nothing but meaningless and worn-out customs.

On the other hand, when this purifying work is carried out and proper progress in the arts takes place, their contribution as a driving force in the development of culture and ethics is great. I believe that this is what Gidayu I had in mind in perfecting his own art and setting up the way of life that we know today as Gidayu-bushi.

My daughter, who was crazy about Latin music before, is now an avid Bunraku fan and is beginning to gain an understanding of its subtleties. Needless to say, her enthusiasm for Bunraku makes me very happy. It is this kind of natural interest in a living, appealing art that is necessary for its continuing vigor and life in the present generation and in the generations to come.

# Chronology

1100   *The Book of Puppeteers* (Kugutsushi Ki) was written by Oe Tadafusa.

1191   Minamoto Yoritomo established the Kamakura shogunate.

1432   Mention of "manipulated lanterns" (*ayatsuri toro*) was made in a book called *Kambun Onki*.

1485   The legend concerning Princess Joruri became popular about this time in the repertoire of wandering troubadours.

1560   About this time the *shamisen* was introduced into Japan from the Ryukyu Islands.

1603   Tokugawa Ieyasu established the Edo shogunate. Okuni began to present the dances which later developed into what we know today as Kabuki.

1610   It is recorded that in August of this year a man from the Ryukyu Islands performed on the *shamisen* in Edo for the first time.

1615   *Joruri* was presented in Edo for the first time by a man named Sugiyama Shichirozaemon, who was later given the name of Tango-no-jo.

1625   *Joruri* based on Buddhist sutras and called *sekkyo joruri* was popular about this time.

1635   *Joruri* was performed at Ise inside the precincts of the Grand Shrine.

1648   Toraya Gendayu began to give regular performances of puppet plays with *joruri* in Edo.

1652   Sugiyama Shichirozaemon went to Kyoto, where he presented a successful season of *joruri* performances. He was recognized by the emperor and received the name Sugiyama Tango-no-jo.

1657   Much of Edo was destroyed in the conflagration known as the Great Fire of the Meireki Era.

1674   The *joruri* narrator Yamamoto Tsunodayu set up a theater at Shijo-gawara in Kyoto.

1675   Uji Kidayu (later known as Kaga-no-jo) presented puppet *joruri* in Kyoto

1677    Gorobei from Tennoji (later known as Takemoto Gidayu) performed as a minor narrator in Uji Kidayu's troupe.

1680    Takemoto Tosa-no-jo and Toraya Eikan performed *joruri* at Nino-maru inside the grounds of Edo Castle.

1683    Uji Kaga-no-jo performed the premier of Chikamatsu Monzaemon's *Heir of the Soga Family* (Yotsugi Soga).

1684    Takemoto Gidayu established the Takemoto-za at Dotombori in Osaka. (Some scholars place this opening in 1685.)

1685    Uji Kaga-no-jo went to Osaka and performed Ihara Saikaku's play *The Calendar* (Koyomi) in competition with Takemoto Gidayu, who performed Chikamatsu's *New Calendar and Lessons Learned by a Wise Woman* (Kenjo no Tenarai Narabi-ni Shin-goyomi).

1686    Chikamatsu Monzaemon wrote *The Successful Kagekiyo* (Shusse Kage-kiyo) expressly for Takemoto Gidayu. Gidayu opened in February at the Takemoto-za with this new play.

1701    In May, Takemoto Gidayu was recognized by the emperor and received the name Takemoto Chikugo-no-jo Fujiwara Hironori.

1703    In May, Chikamatsu Monzaemon's first play written in his new *sewa-mono* style, called *The Double Suicide at Sonezaki* (Sonezaki Shinju) was premiered at the Takemoto-za. The Toyotake-za, founded by Echizen-no-shojo, opened at Dotombori in Osaka.

1705    The Toyotake-za was closed down.

1706    Wakadayu opened the Toyotake-za once more toward the end of the year and hired Ki no Kaion as playwright.

1707    Chikamatsu's *Drumming of the Waves at Horikawa* (Horikawa Nami no Tsuzumi) was performed at the Takemoto-za. A Kyoto narrator named Itchu developed the style of *joruri* called Itchu-bushi about this time.

1711    Uji Kaga-no-jo died in January at the age of seventy-six. Chikamatsu's *Messenger from Hades* (Meido no Hikyaku) was premiered at the Takemoto-za.

1714    On September 10, Takemoto Gidayu died at the age of sixty-three.

1715    Chikamatsu Monzaemon's *Battle of Kokusenya* (Kokusenya Kassen) opened at the Takemoto-za under the management of Takeda Izumo and began a run of seventeen months.

1724    Chikamatsu Monzaemon died on November 22 at the age of seventy-one.

1726    In April, *The Tale of Hojo Tokiyori* (Hojo Tokiyori Ki), a joint work of Nishizawa Ippu and Namiki Sosuke, opened at the Toyotake-za and was such a great success that it put the theater back on its feet financially.

1734    In May, the puppeteer Tatsumatsu Hachirobei died. In October,

*The Tale of Ashiya Doman Ouchi* (Ashiya Doman Ouchi Kagami) was presented at the Takemoto-za. In this production Yoshida Bunzaburo, for the first time in history, presented puppets handled by three puppeteers each.

1742   In October, Ki no Kaion, the playwright of the Toyotake-za, died at the age of seventy-nine.

1745   In July, *The Tale of the Summer Festival at Osaka* (Natsu Matsuri Naniwa Kagami), a joint work of Namiki Senryu (formerly known as Sosuke), Miyoshi Shoraku, and Takeda Ko-izumo (Izumo II), was premiered at the Takemoto-za under the direction of Yoshida Bunzaburo. Bunzaburo made further improvements in his three-man puppet-handling system. He also gained a new level of realism by using real water and mud in the famous murder scene of the last act.

1746   In August, *The Tale of Sugawara Michizane* (Sugawara Denju Tenarai Kagami), a joint work of Takeda Izumo I, Namiki Senryu, and Miyoshi Shoraku, was premiered at the Takemoto-za.

1747   *Yoshitsune and the Thousand Cherry Trees* (Yoshitsune Sembon-zakura), a joint work of Takeda Izumo II, Namiki Senryu, and Miyoshi Shoraku, was premiered at the Takemoto-za.

1748   In August, *The Faithful Forty-seven* (Kanadehon Chushingura), a joint work of Izumo II, Senryu, and Shoraku, was premiered at the Takemoto-za. On the opening day of this play the narrator Takemoto Konodayu and the puppeteer Yoshida Bunzaburo had a quarrel which resulted in Konodayu's moving to the Toyotake-za.

1749   In July, a joint work of Izumo II, Senryu, and Shoraku entitled *The Diary Concerning Two Butterflies in the Gay Quarters* (Futatsu Chocho Kuruwa no Nikki) was premiered at the Takemoto-za.

1756   Takeda Izumo II died on November 4, and the Takemoto-za entered a period of weak management.

1760   Yoshida Bunzaburo died on January 19.

1764   Toyotake Echizen-no-shojo died at the age of eighty-three.

1765   The Toyotake-za closed its doors forever.

1767   The Takemoto-za was converted into a Kabuki theater.

1769   The Takemoto-za was reopened as a Gidayu-bushi theater.

1771   In January, *Proper Upbringing of a Young Lady at Mount Imose* (Imose-yama Onna Teikin), a joint work of Chikamatsu Hanji and Matsuda Bakura, was premiered at the Takemoto-za.

1772   The Takemoto-za closed its doors forever.

1780   Chikamatsu Hanji wrote *The New Ballad Singer* (Shimpan Utazaimon).

1783   Chikamatsu Hanji died on February 4 at the age of fifty-eight.

1805    Uemura Bunraku-ken formed the troupe which later developed into the Bunraku-za.

1810    Uemura Bunraku-ken died.

1811    Uemura Bunraku-ken II established a theater on the grounds of the Inari Shrine in Osaka.

1842    The government promulgated a law absolutely forbidding performances of any kind in the precincts of temples and shrines. The Gidayu-bushi theater in the precincts of the Inari Shrine in Osaka was closed down.

1857    The theater at the Inari Shrine in Osaka was once more opened and presented Gidayu-bushi.

1868    The Meiji Restoration was carried out.

1871    In January, under the auspices of the Osaka city government, the Gidayu-bushi troupe was moved from the precincts of the Inari Shrine to another part of Osaka called Matsushima. The new theater was named the Bunraku-za. The main performers were the narrator Takemoto Harudayu V and the puppeteer Yoshida Tamazo.

1877    Takemoto Harudayu V died in July at the age of sixty-nine. Takemoto Jitsudayu IV (later known as Nagatodayu) took over as main performer.

1878    Toyotake Koutsubodayu I died in February.

1884    In January, the Hikoroku-za was opened in the precincts of the Inari Shrine in Osaka. In August, the *shamisen* player Dampei II left the Bunraku-za and joined Takemoto Osumidayu III as accompanist at the Hikoroku-za.

1887    Uemura Bunraku-o (Bunraku-ken II) died in February at the age of seventy-four.

1893    The Hikoroku-za was closed down in September.

1894    In March, the Inari-za opened with Toyozawa Dampei II, Takemoto Yadayu V, and Takemoto Osumidayu III as its main performers.

1898    Toyozawa Dampei II died in April at the age of seventy-four. The Inari-za closed down in June.

1903    In May, Takemoto Harudayu VI (Koshijidayu) was recognized by the emperor and received the name Matsumoto Settsu-no-taisho. The celebrated Kabuki actors Onoe Kikugoro V and Ichikawa Danjuro IX died.

1905    In January, the puppeteer Yoshida Oyatama (Tamazo I) died at the age of seventy-five.

1909    The Bunraku-za came under the management of the Shochiku Company, beginning in March.

1910    Kiritake Monjuro I died in August.

1913    Takemoto Osumidayu III died in July at the age of sixty.

1917 Takemoto Settsu-no-taisho died in October at the age of eighty-one.

1924 Koshijidayu III died in March at the age of fifty-nine.

1926 The Bunraku-za burned down in November.

1930 The new Bunraku-za was opened in January at Yotsuhashi in Osaka with Takemoto Tsudayu III, Takemoto Tosadayu VI, Toyotake Koutsubodayu II (Yamashiro-no-shojo), Yoshida Eiza, and Yoshida Bungoro III as its chief performers.

1941 Takemoto Tosadayu VI died in April at the age of seventy-eight. Takemoto Tsudayu III died in May at the age of seventy-two.

1945 In March, the Bunraku-za burned down once again. In December, Yoshida Eiza died at the age of seventy-three.

1946 The Bunraku-za was rebuilt and opened in February.

1947 In January, Toyotake Koutsubodayu II was granted the name Toyotake Yamashiro-no-shojo by the household of Prince Chichibu.

1949 In March, the Bunraku-za split into two groups, one in the form of a union headed by Kiritake Monjuro II and called the Mitsuwa-kai, the other an antiunion group centering around Yamashiro-no-shojo and Yoshida Bungoro III and called the Chinami-kai.

1956 The Shochiku Company built the new Bunraku-za (present Asahi-za) at Dotombori in Osaka.

1963 Yoshida Naniwa-no-jo (Bungoro III) died in February at the age of ninety-three. In April, the Mitsuwa-kai and the Chinami-kai were once more brought together, and the Bunraku Association was formed. Since that time, the association has been supported by the National Commission for the Protection of Cultural Properties, the Osaka prefectural and municipal governments, and NHK (Japan Broadcasting Corporation).

1966 The new National Theater, which contains a small theater designed especially for Bunraku performances, was opened in Tokyo.

1967 Toyotake Wakadayu X died in April at the age of seventy-eight. In the same month Toyotake Yamashiro-no-shojo died at the age of eighty-eight.

# Commentaries
# on the Illustrations

1. The faithful wife Osono in the famous Wineshop scene (Sakaya no dan) from *The Woman in a Gaudy Dance Costume* (Hadesugata Onna Maiginu).

2. Sadaka and Daihanji confront each other after the death of their children in the Mountain scene (Yama no dan) from *Proper Upbringing of a Young Lady at Mount Imose* (Imose-yama Onna Teikin). Sadaka has beheaded her daughter Hinadori to save her from a hateful marriage. Daihanji's son Koganosuke, in love with Hinadori, has committed ritual suicide. From left to right: Sadaka: Kiritake Monjuro; Daihanji: Kiritake Kamematsu; Koganosuke: Toyomatsu Seijuro.

3. Kinezo (right) and Ousu (left) pound rice to make dumplings in the light comic dance *The Dumpling Sellers* (Dango Uri). Kinezo: Yoshida Kodama; Ousu: Kiritake Monju.

4. The servant Tarokaja catches a very ugly wife for himself with his master's magic fishhook in *Fishing for a Wife* (Tsuri Onna). Tarokaja (right): Kiritake Kanjuro; wife (left): Toyomatsu Seijuro.

5. In the Ichiriki Teahouse scene (Ichiriki Chaya no dan) of *The Faithful Forty-seven* (Kanadehon Chushingura) the courtesan Okaru uses her mirror to read a secret letter at the same time that Yuranosuke is reading it in the adjoining room, while the spy Kudayu, hidden under the veranda, also tries to discover its contents. Okaru: Yoshida Eiza; Yuranosuke: Yoshida Tamasuke.

6. The courtesan Yugiri in *Yugiri at the Straits of Awa* (Yugiri Awa no Naruto).

7. The villainess Yashio, in the third act of *The Perfume of the Old Bush Clover* (Meiboku Sendai Hagi), gloats over the body of the murdered boy Semmatsu. Yashio: Kiritake Monjuro.

8-9. The medieval warriors Abe Sadato (left) and his brother Muneto (right) in *On the Adachi Plain in*

213

*Oshu* (Oshu Adachigahara). Abe Sadato: Kiritake Monjuro; Abe Muneto: Kiritake Kanjuro.

10–11. Two episodes from the celebrated sixth act—The Temple School (Terakoya)—of *The Tale of Sugawara Michizane* (Sugawara Denju Tenarai Kagami). At right, Matsuo orders his wife Chiyo to restrain her grief over the death of their son Kotaro, whose life has been sacrificed to save that of their lord's son. At left, Chiyo, dressed in mourning clothes, prepares to escort her son's body to the funeral rites. Matsuo: Yoshida Tatsugoro; Chiyo: Kiritake Monjuro.

12. Princess Yaegaki is possessed by the spirit of a fox and steals a valuable helmet in the Fox Fires scene (Kitsunebi no dan) from *Twenty-four Expressions of Filial Love* (Honcho Nijushiko). Princess Yaegaki: Kiritake Monjuro.

13. Gappo stabs his wayward daughter Tsuji in the climactic scene of *Gappo of Sesshu and His Daughter Tsuji* (Sesshu Gappo ga Tsuji). Tsuji: Kiritake Monjuro; Gappo: Kiritake Kanjuro.

14. The warrior Takechi Mitsuhide in the Amagasaki scene (Amagasaki no dan) from *The Picture Book of the Taiko Tales* (Ehon Taiko Ki). Mitsuhide: Kiritake Kamematsu.

15. Misao, wife of the warrior Takechi Mitsuhide, in the Moon-flower Trellis scene (Yugaodana no dan) from *The Picture Book of the Taiko Tales* (Ehon Taiko Ki). Misao: Kiritake Monjuro.

16–18. In the Kawazura Mansion scene (Kawazura Hogan Yakata no dan) of *Yoshitsune and the Thousand Cherry Trees* (Yoshitsune Sembon-zakura), Tadanobu, the warrior who has accompanied the heroine Shizuka on her trip to meet her lover Yoshitsune, reveals that he is actually a fox in disguise. Yoshitsune (right): Yoshida Gyokusho; Shizuka (center): Yoshida Tamagoro; Tadanobu and fox (left): Yoshida Eiza.

19. In the same scene as the preceding one, the fox (Tadanobu) flies happily away after having recovered the magic drum made from the skin of his parents. Fox: Yoshida Eiza.

20–23. Four episodes from the Sushi Shop scene (Sushiya no dan) of *Yoshitsune and the Thousand Cherry Trees* (Yoshitsune Sembon-zakura). 20: Gonta, wearing a towel as headgear, is on his way to his parents' *sushiya* (a shop selling a mixture of cooked rice and other foods) to try to talk them out of some money. 21: He enters from the back of the shop. 22: He demands money from his mother. 23: He runs off with the *sushi* tub which he thinks contains the money he stole from his parents' cashbox but which actually contains the head of a dead samurai. Gonta:

Yoshida Tamasuke; mother: Yoshida Tsuneji.

24. Yuranosuke, in the Ichiriki Teahouse scene (Ichiriki Chaya no dan) of *The Faithful Forty-seven* (Kanadehon Chushingura), discovers the spy Kudayu, who is hiding under the veranda. Yuranosuke: Yoshida Tamasuke.

25. In the scene known as Bloodshed in the Palace (Denchu Ninjo no dan) from *The Faithful Forty-seven* (Kanadehon Chushingura), Enya Hangan, brandishing his sword, attempts to rush after Moronao, who has viciously insulted him, but is held back by Honzo and his retainers. Enya Hangan: Toyomatsu Seijuro; Honzo: Yoshida Tamaichi.

26. Fukashichi stabs Omiwa in the Palace scene (Goten no dan) from *Proper Upbringing of a Young Lady at Mount Imose* (Imoseyama Onna Teikin). Omiwa: Kiritake Monjuro; Fukashichi: Yoshida Tamasuke.

27. Otani falls at her husband Masaemon's feet when she catches up with him in the mountains in the Okazaki scene (Okazaki no dan) from *The Trip Through the Iga Mountains* (Iga-goe Dochu Sugoroku). Masaemon: Yoshida Eiza; Otani: Kiritake Monjuro.

28–29. Two episodes from the Wineshop scene (Sakaya no dan) in *The Wonan in a Gaudy Dance Costume* (Hadesugata Onna Maiginu). 28: Osono dusts a lamp

during her famous monologue about her erring husband Hanshichi. 29: Hanshichi and his mistress Sankatsu make the decision to die together. Osono: Yoshida Eiza; Hanshichi: Yoshida Tamayuki; Sankatsu: Yoshida Bunsho.

30. Kokan walks alone at night in the Night Morning-Glory scene (Yoru no Asagao no dan) from *The Double Suicide on the First Day Ice Was on the Sword* (Shinju Yaiba wa Kori no Tsuitachi). Kokan: Yoshida Eiza.

31. Osome and her lover Hisamatsu sadly discuss their fate in the Nozaki Village scene (Nozakimura no dan) of *The New Ballad Singer* (Shimpan Utazaimon). Osome: Yoshida Minosuke; Hisamatsu: Yoshida Bunsho.

32–34. Three episodes from the Horikawa Monkey Trainer scene (Horikawa Sarumawashi no dan) in *A Recent Story of Rivalry in Kawara* (Chikagoro Kawara no Tatehiki). 32: The monkey trainer Yojiro, elder brother of the heroine Oshun, shoulders a broom. 33: The hero Dembei comes to visit Oshun to tell her of his plan to die alone because they cannot be together. 34: Yojiro's mother tries to comfort Dembei. Yojiro: Kiritake Monjuro; Oshun: Kiritake Kamematsu; Dembei: Kiritake Kanjuro; Yojiro's mother: Yoshida Kunihide.

35. In the Window in Yawata Village scene (Yawata-sato Hikimado no dan) from *The Diary Concern-*

ing *Two Butterflies in the Gay Quarters* (Futatsu Chocho Kuruwa no Nikki), the murderer Nuregami Chogoro returns to his mother's house to bid her farewell. Nuregami Chogoro: Kiritake Kanjuro.

36. In the same scene as the preceding one Nambo Jujihei prepares a cord for binding a criminal. Nambo Jujihei: Yoshida Tatsugoro.

37–38. Two episodes from the Warm Kotatsu and Autumn Rain scene (Shigure Kotatsu no dan) in *The Double Suicide at Ten no Amijima* (Shinju Ten no Amijima). 37: The paper merchant Jihei warms himself in the *kotatsu* (quilt-covered charcoal pit) while discussing with his wife Osan the problem of his love affair with the courtesan Koharu. 38: The villainous Edoya Zenroku reads a letter. Osan: Yoshida Tamao; Jihei: Kiritake Monjuro; Edoya Zenroku: Kiritake Monya.

39–40. Two scenes from *The Miracle at Tsubosaka* (Tsubosaka Reigen Ki). 39: The blind man Sawaichi prepares to fling himself over a cliff in the Tsubosaka Temple scene (Tsubosaka-dera no dan). 40: Sawaichi quarrels with his wife Osato in the scene at Sawaichi's house (Sawaichi Uchi no dan). Sawaichi: Kiritake Kanjuro; Osato: Kiritake Monjuro.

41–44. Two episodes from *The Tale of the Summer Festival in Osaka* (Natsu Matsuri Naniwa Kagami). 41–43: Danshichi, the tattooed hero of the play, murders his rascally

father-in-law Giheiji while a festival procession passes through a neighboring street in the Naga-machi scene (Naga-machi Ura no dan). 44: Danshichi fights the police as he tries to escape over the rooftops in the Tajima-machi scene (Tajima-machi Danshichi Uchi no dan). Danshichi: Kiritake Kanjuro.

45. The courtesan Akoya in *The Chronicle of the Battle Helmet at Dannoura* (Dannoura Kabuto Gunki). Akoya: Kiritake Monjuro.

46. Early puppeteers. Detail from a painting depicting various customs and entertainments. Owned by the Emman-in, Otsu, Shiga Prefecture, and classed as an Important Cultural Property.

47. Early hand-puppet show. Detail from a six-panel folding screen depicting scenes in and around Kyoto. Owned by Tammachi Juro, Tokyo.

48. Early puppeteers. Detail from a six-panel screen by Kano Eitoku (1543–90) depicting scenes in and around Kyoto. Owned by Uesugi Takanori, Yonezawa, Yamagata Prefecture, and classed as an Important Cultural Property.

49. Early string-operated marionettes. Painting on wooden sliding doors dated 1652. Owned by Yamada Soi, Kamakura, Kanagawa Prefecture.

50. Puppet theater of the Keicho era (1596–1610). Detail from a

six-panel screen depicting scenes in and around Kyoto and painted about 1614. Owned by the Tokyo National Museum and classed as an Important Cultural Property.

51. Puppet theater of the Keicho era (1596–1610). Detail from a two-panel screen showing scenes at Shijo-gawara in Kyoto. Owned by Domoto Shiro, Kyoto, and classed as an Important Cultural Property.

52. The Kabuki actor Sanogawa Ichimatsu performing as a puppeteer. Woodblock print by Okumura Masanobu (1691–1768).

53. *Oshizumo* puppets: the oldest puppet form in existence in Japan. These puppets are used in the festival of the Koyo Shrine at Nakatsu, Oita Prefecture.

54. *Noroma* puppet head: Ohana (comic woman). Owned by Tsuruma Yoshio, Niigata Prefecture.

55. *Ko-joruri* puppet head: Ibaragi Doji (demon). Owned by Tsuruma Yoshio, Niigata Prefecture.

56. Awa puppet head: Kaminari (god of thunder).

57. Kuruma puppet head: *waka-otoko* (young man).

58. Dance puppet used in the festival of the Koyo Shrine, Nakatsu, Oita Prefecture.

59. *Aizumo* puppet used in the festival of the Kohyo Shrine, Chikugo County, Fukuoka Prefecture.

60–61. *Ko-joruri* puppet heads. 60: Kintoki (a folk hero). 61: Odai (woman). Owned by Tsuruma Yoshio, Niigata Prefecture.

62. Early puppeteers. Detail from a screen painting depicting customs of the Momoyama period (1573–1602). Owned by the Kyoto Prefectural Library.

63. *Biwa-hoshi* (itinerant narrator-priest) and attendant (foreground). Detail from a painting depicting the arts and crafts of the Edo period (1603–1868). Owned by Nakajima Tsunehiro, Tokyo.

64. Princess Joruri. Drawing from the *Twelve-Step Joruri Book* owned by the Theater Museum of Waseda University, Tokyo.

65. Princess Joruri. Drawing from the Saga-bon *Twelve-Step Joruri Book,* a history of *joruri.*

66. Puppet performance in front of a dry-goods shop. Detail from a painting depicting Japanese customs.

67. Puppet play in the Kan'ei era (1624–43). Detail from a folding screen depicting customs of the day.

68. Early puppet theater. Detail from a six-panel folding screen depicting scenes in and around Kyoto. Owned by Tammachi Juro, Tokyo.

69. Program for a puppet performance during the Kambun era (1661–72). Owned by the Tenri Library, Tenri, Nara Prefecture.

70. Dressing room of Yamamoto Tosa-no-jo's troupe. Part of a collection of drawings depicting various types of education and training.

71. Caricature depicting the exploits of the ancient hero Kimpira, the main character in the early form of narration called Kimpira-bushi. From a collection of vocal music.

72. In and around a puppet theater of the Edo period (1603–1868). The interior of the theater is seen at top right. At bottom right is a tea shop. Detail from a picture scroll showing customs of the times. Owned by the Suntory Art Gallery, Tokyo.

73. Drawing of a performance by Uji Kaga-no-jo's troupe in the late seventeenth or early eighteenth century.

74. Performance by Inoue Harima-no-jo's troupe. Illustration from a seventeenth-century book concerning the descendants of the medieval hero Minamoto Yorimitsu (Raiko).

75. Portrait of Takemoto Gidayu (1651–1714).

76. Portrait of Chikamatsu Monzaemon (1653–1724). Owned by Okada Rihei, Itami, Hyogo Prefecture.

77. Eighteenth-century drawing picturing the premiere performance of *The Tale of Hojo Tokiyori* (Hojo Tokiyori Ki). From an early book about puppets and joruri called *Konjiki Ayatsuri Hendaiki.*

78. Drawing of the Toyotake-za (left) and the Takemoto-za (right) from an eighteenth-century book on the history of the Toyotake-za.

79. Eighteenth-century drawing of some of the stage tricks devised by Takeda Izumo I.

80. Drawing from an eighteenth-century document picturing a performance of *The Double Suicide at Sonezaki* (Sonezaki Shinju) with Tatsumatsu Hachirobei as puppeteer and Takemoto Chikugo-no-jo (Gidayu I) as narrator.

81. Drawing of a *joruri* theater during the Kyowa era (1801–3).

82. Eighteenth-century drawing of early three-man puppets.

83. Drawing from a program for a puppet show during the Kan'en era (1748–50).

84. Drawing from a program for a puppet show around the middle of the Edo period (1603–1868), showing Yoshida Bunzaburo I on the right.

85. Program for the premiere performance of *Proper Upbringing of a Young Lady at Mount Imose* (Imoseyama Onna Teikin) in 1771.

86. Last pages, with colophon, of original text of *The Ghost at the Yaguchi Ferry Crossing* (Shinrei Yaguchi no Watashi), first produced in 1770.

87. Cover (right) and specimen page (left) from the original text of *The Tale of Sugawara Michizane* (Sugawara Denju Tenarai Kagami), first produced in 1746.

88. Page from the original text of *The Faithful Forty-seven* (Kanadehon Chushingura), first produced in 1748.

89. Page from the original text of *The Battle of Kokusenya* (Kokusenya Kassen), first produced in 1715.

90. Woodblock print of the late Edo period (late eighteenth to mid-nineteenth century) picturing the Edo theater district called Saruwaka-machi (near the present Asakusa district in Tokyo).

91. Woodblock print of the late Edo period (late eighteenth to mid-nineteenth century) showing a puppet *joruri* performance. Owned by the Theater Museum of Waseda University, Tokyo.

92. Bunraku program of the Meiji era (1868–1912). Owned by the Theater Museum of Waseda University, Tokyo.

93. Takemoto Koshijidayu IV as narrator and Nozawa Kizaemon II as *shamisen* accompanist in a performance of *The Miracle at Tsubosaka* (Tsubosaka Reigen Ki).

94. Acting area of the stage during a performance of *Three Generations at Kamakura* (Kamakura Sandai Ki). Puppeteers (left to right):

Yoshida Kodama, Yoshida Gyokusho, Kiritake Monju.

95. Puppet heads in the dressing room of the National Theater, Tokyo.

96. Preparation of a puppet head for a performance, National Theater, Tokyo.

97. Bunshichi head. Used for middle-aged male roles.

98. Musume head. Used for young female roles.

99. Puppets in the dressing room ready for a performance.

100. View of entrance to the National Theater, the present Tokyo home of Bunraku.

101. Interior of the small hall at the National Theater, Tokyo, during a performance of *The Miracle at Tsubosaka* (Tsubosaka Reigen Ki). Narrator: Koshijidayu IV. *Shamisen* accompanist: Kizaemon II. Puppeteers: Kiritake Kanjuro (Sawaichi) and Kiritake Monjuro (Osato).

102. Puppeteer waiting in the wings for his entrance cue.

103. *Tozai* announcement which opens each act and scene of Bunraku. The announcer uses a pair of wooden clappers to attract the attention of the audience.

104. Stage viewed from the wings, with puppet and props in the foreground.

105. Puppeteers during a performance as seen from the wings.

106. Performance viewed from the wings. The stagehand at right strikes a board with wooden blocks to produce sound effects which accent dramatic moments in the action.

107. Sceneshifter awaiting his cue during a performance.

108. *Kakeai:* the use of numerous narrators and *shamisen* players in one play or scene. The play in this case is the famous *Subscription List* (Kanjincho).

109. View of the stage from above during a performance of the Amagasaki scene (Amagasaki no dan) from *The Picture Book of the Taiko Tales* (Ehon Taiko Ki). Takechi Jujiro, armed for battle, bids farewell to his sweetheart Hatsugiku. Jujiro: Yoshida Tamagoro; Hatsugiku: Yoshida Minosuke.

110–13. The narrator Tsunadayu VIII in a performance of the Naga-machi scene (Naga-machi Ura no dan) from *The Tale of the Summer Festival in Osaka* (Natsu Matsuri Naniwa Kagami).

114–15. The *shamisen* player Kizaemon II in a performance of the Tsubosaka Temple scene (Tsubosaka-dera no dan) from *The Miracle at Tsubosaka* (Tsubosaka Reigen Ki).

116–17. Two views of the puppeteers' dressing room in the National Theater, Tokyo.

118. Kiritake Monjuro preparing a puppet for a performance.

119. Puppets and their storage baskets.

120. Body and head of a male puppet mounted on its dressing-room stand.

121. Body of a female puppet with the undercollar in place.

122. Base and head of a female puppet mounted on its dressing-room stand. The pin in the lower lip serves to secure objects which are held in the mouth.

123. Puppet hand with four fingers movable as a single unit.

124. Puppet hand with movable wrist and thumb and four fingers movable as a single unit.

125. Puppet hand with movable fingers and wrist.

126. Puppet hand movable only at the wrist.

127. Puppet hand designed for holding a fan.

128. Puppet hand with plectrum for use in playing the lute (*biwa*).

129. Fully jointed puppet hand closed into a fist.

130. Fully jointed puppet hand opened wide.

131–32. Manipulation of movable eyebrows in a male-puppet head.

133–35. Manipulation of a male-puppet leg.

136-37. Two views of the master craftsman Oe Minosuke carving a puppet head.

138. Danshichi head. Used for evil middle-aged male roles.

139. Danshichi head of the O-Danshichi type, with movable eyebrows and mouth.

140. Bunshichi head with movable eyebrows and mouth. Used for middle-aged male roles.

141. Waka-otoko head. Used for young male roles.

142. Genta head with movable eyebrows. Used for young male roles.

143. Komei head. Used for middle-aged male roles.

144. Kebiishi head with movable eyebrows. Used for young male roles.

145. Oniwaka head. Used for young male roles.

146. Yokambei head. Used for evil young male roles.

147. Darasuke head. Used for evil young male roles.

148. Matabei head. Used for male clown roles. The pin in the tongue serves for securing objects which are held in the mouth.

149. Ojuto head. Used for evil aged male roles.

150. Torao head. Used for evil aged male roles.

151. Masamune head. Used for aged male roles.

152. Kiichi head. Used for aged male roles.

153. Shiratayu head. Used for aged male roles.

154. Takeuji head. Used for aged male roles.

155. Sadanoshin head. Used for aged male roles.

156. Yashio head. Used for evil middle-aged female roles.

157. Keisei head. Used for roles of beautiful courtesans.

158. Baba head. Used for aged female roles.

159. Ofuku head. Used for female clown roles.

160. Fuke-oyama head. Used for middle-aged female roles. The pin in the lower lip serves to secure articles which are held in the mouth.

161-62. Gabu head. Used for roles of demons disguised as beautiful women who reveal their true form at the climax of a play. The lower part of the face drops to open a mouth filled with pointed teeth; the eyes change to gleaming golden balls; and horns spring up from the top of the head.

163. Kagekiyo head. Used only for the role of Kagekiyo, the defeated Heike warrior.

164.   Tsume head. Used for minor female roles.

165.   Tsume head. Used for minor male roles.

166.   Koyaku head. Used for male child roles.

167.   Koyaku head. Used for female child roles.

168–69.  Nashi-wari (lit., "split pear") head. Used for minor char-acters whose heads are split open during sword fights.

170.   Chari head, *detchi* style. Used for roles of comic young male servants.

171.   Chari head, *sammaime* style. Used for comic male roles.

172.   Myorin head. Used for comic nun roles.

173.   The Asahi-za at Dotombori, present home of Bunraku in Osaka.

The "weathermark"
identifies this book as having been
planned, designed, and produced at
the Tokyo offices of
John Weatherhill, Inc.
7–6–13 Roppongi, Minato-ku, Tokyo 106
Book design and typography by Ronald V. Bell
Layout of photographs by Tanko-sha, Kyoto
Composition by Samwha Printing Co., Ltd., Seoul
Color and gravure plates engraved and printed by
Dai Nippon Printing Co., Ltd., Tokyo
Text printed by Kinmei Printing Co., Ltd., Tokyo
Binding by Okamoto Binderies, Tokyo
Set in 11-point Monotype Baskerville
with hand-set Bulmer for display